LINCOLN

A Book of Quotations

DOVER THRIFT EDITIONS

Edited by
Bob Blaisdell

DOVER PUBLICATI
MINEOLA, NEW

DOVER THRIFT EDITIONS

GENERAL EDITOR: SUSAN L. RATTINER
EDITOR OF THIS VOLUME: JIM MILLER

Bibliographical Note

Lincoln: A Book of Quotations, first published by Dover Publications, Inc., in 2016, is a republication in a new format of the text from *Abraham Lincoln's Wit and Wisdom*, originally published by Dover in 2013.

International Standard Book Number

ISBN-13: 978-0-486-80607-5
ISBN-10: 0-486-80607-3

Manufactured in the United States by LSC Communications
80607303   2020
www.doverpublications.com

NOTE

It is the strangest and yet the fittest thing in the jumble of human vicissitudes, that he, out of so many millions, unlooked for, unselected by any intelligible process that could be based upon his genuine qualities, unknown to those who chose him, and unsuspected of what endowments may adapt him for his tremendous responsibility, should have found the way open for him to fling his lank personality into the chair of state,—where, I presume, it was his first impulse to throw his legs on the council-table, and tell the Cabinet Ministers a story.

—*Nathaniel Hawthorne, July 1862*

America's most famous and most mythologized man is, even with the myth stripped away, probably one of our greatest presidents and certainly one of our most remarkable and representative men. "It is very strange that I," he reflected near the end of the Civil War, "a boy brought up in the woods, and seeing, as it were, but little of the world, should be drifted into the very apex of this great event." How strange (and fortunate), indeed, it was that he, born in 1809 in the backwoods of Kentucky, raised on the frontier of Indiana, a self-educated lawyer in Illinois, found his way to state and then national politics and became, to his own amazement, the president of the United States at its moment of deepest crisis: the secession of rebel states over the issue of the extension of America's most vile institution, slavery. He steered America, "a house divided," as he famously described it, through its war upon itself, its war of brothers and families, and he was assassinated at its end in 1865. Only hours before he was fatally shot, he envisioned the

peaceful and healing aftermath of the national and personal catas-
trophe, saying to his wife Mary, "We must both be more cheerful
in the future. Between the war and the loss of our darling Willie,
we have both been very miserable." (One of their young sons had
died of disease during the war.)

It is not a myth that Lincoln was wise and witty; his powerful
and conversational phrasings continually demonstrate the workings
of a lively, quick, and sensitive mind. "It is very common in this
country to find great facility of expression and less common to find
great lucidity of thought," he told a British journalist. "The combination of the two in one person is very uncommon; but whenever you do find it, you have a great man." Lincoln himself devel-
oped that "combination," and he rose to become our "great man."
As a public man, he seems to have been generally consistent in his
views on slavery, the law, and morality. Though I have distributed
his statements into various broad categories, few of the quotations
could not have found an appropriate home in another category or
two. I have tried to limit the selection to quotations that were
characteristic rather than odd or exceptional, and to rely on those
statements that are more or less self-explanatory. I have arranged
the quotations chronologically within their categories, with the
undatable remarks placed thematically.

Most of the designated "remarks" (his statements recorded not in
writing but in conversation) should be taken as secondhand. To help
determine the reliability of such remarks, I have depended on the
scholarship of Lincoln experts. During his presidency, Lincoln became famous as the purported author of many anecdotes he had
never even told, much less created. "I do generally remember a good
story when I hear it," he told a friend during the Civil War, "but I
never did invent anything original; I am only a retail dealer." He
became America's model of the folksy joke-teller in spite of this, so
I have included a few of the jokes he seems to have actually recounted.

While a fine writer, Lincoln was never a good speller, nor did he
ever get around to memorizing rules of punctuation. "With educated people, I suppose, punctuation is a matter of rule; with me it
is a matter of feeling," he told a friend. "But I must say that I have
a great respect for the semicolon; it's a very useful little chap." For
the sake of clarity, I have corrected his punctuation and spelling.
For this project (and its earlier, shorter incarnation in 2005), I thank

my father, Dr. F. William Blaisdell, for the loan of his Civil War books and his suggestions of examples of Lincoln's humor, and my son, Max, for his help in tagging the hundreds of quotations from *The Collected Works*. Max's recent interest in collecting quotations about Lincoln by his contemporaries led to the Appendix, in this new edition, of observations and opinions on Lincoln's character by his friends and foes.

—Bob Blaisdell
New York City
September 2012

CONTENTS

AMERICA

We find ourselves in the peaceful possession of the fairest portion of earth as regards extent of territory, fertility of soil, and salubrity of climate. We find ourselves under the government of a system of political institutions conducing more essentially to the ends of civil and religious liberty than any of which the history of former times tells us. We, when mounting the stage of existence, found ourselves the legal inheritors of these fundamental blessings. We toiled not in the acquirement of establishment of them—they are a legacy bequeathed us by a *once* hardy, brave, and patriotic but *now* lamented and departed race of ancestors. Theirs was a task (and nobly they performed it) to possess themselves, and through themselves, us, of this goodly land; and to uprear upon its hills and valleys a political edifice of liberty and equal rights; 'tis ours only, to transmit these, the former, unprofaned by the foot of an invader; the latter, undecayed by the lapse of time and untorn by usurpation, to the latest generation that fate shall permit the world to know.
    —*"The Perpetuation of Our Political Institutions": Address before the Young Men's Lyceum of Springfield, Illinois, January 27, 1838*

֍

At what point shall we expect the approach of danger? By what means shall we fortify against it?—Shall we expect some transatlantic military giant to step the ocean and crush us at a blow? Never!—All the armies of Europe, Asia and Africa combined, with all the treasure of the earth (our own excepted) in their military chest, with a Buonaparte for a commander, could not by force take a drink from the Ohio or make a track on the Blue Ridge in a trial of a thousand years.

1

At what point then is the approach of danger to be expected? I answer, if it ever reach us, it must spring up amongst us. It cannot come from abroad. If destruction be our lot, we must ourselves be its author and finisher. As a nation of freemen, we must live through all time or die by suicide.

— *"The Perpetuation of Our Political Institutions": Address before the Young Men's Lyceum of Springfield, Illinois, January 27, 1838*

✎

We are a great empire. We are eighty years old. We stand at once the wonder and admiration of the whole world, and we must enquire what it is that has given us so much prosperity, and we shall understand that to give up that one thing would be to give up all future prosperity. This cause is that every man can make himself. It has been said that such a race of prosperity has been run nowhere else. ... we see a people who, while they boast of being free, keep their fellow beings in bondage.

—*Speech, Kalamazoo, Michigan, August 27, 1856*

✎

If the great American people will only keep their temper, on both sides of the line, the troubles will come to an end, and the question which now distracts the country will be settled just as surely as all other difficulties of like character which have originated in this government have been adjusted. Let the people on both sides keep their self-possession, and just as other clouds have cleared away in the time, so will this, and this great nation shall continue to prosper as heretofore.

—*Speech, Pittsburgh, Pennsylvania, February 15, 1861*

✎

A nation may be said to consist of its territory, its people, and its laws. The territory is the only part which is of certain durability. "One generation passeth away, and another generation cometh, but the earth abideth forever." It is of the first importance to duly consider and estimate this ever-enduring part. That portion of the earth's surface which is owned and inhabited by the people of the

United States is well adapted to be the home of one national family, and it is not well adapted for two or more. Its vast extent and its variety of climate and productions are of advantage in this age for one people, whatever they might have been in former ages. Steam, telegraphs, and intelligence have brought these to be an advantageous combination for one united people.

—Annual Message to Congress, December 1, 1862

৯

Our national strife springs not from our permanent part; not from the land we inhabit; not from our national homestead. There is no possible severing of this, but would multiply, and not mitigate, evils among us. In all its adaptations and aptitudes, it demands union, and abhors separation. In fact, it would, ere long, force reunion, however much of blood and treasure the separation might have cost. Our strife pertains to ourselves—to the passing generations of men; and it can, without convulsion, be hushed forever from the passing of one generation.

—Annual Message to Congress, December 1, 1862

৯

Four score and seven years ago our fathers brought forth, on this continent, a new nation, conceived in Liberty, and dedicated to the proposition that all men are created equal.

—Gettysburg Address, at the dedication of the cemetery at Gettysburg,
Pennsylvania, November 19, 1863

৯

Nowhere in the world is presented a government of so much liberty and equality. To the humblest and poorest amongst us are held out the highest privileges and positions. The present moment finds me at the White House, yet there is as good a chance for your children as there was for my father's.

—Speech to 148th Ohio Regiment, August 31, 1864

৯

EDUCATION AND ADVICE FOR THE YOUNG

Upon the system of education, not presuming to dictate any plan or system respecting it, I can only say that I view it as the most important subject which we as a people can be engaged in. That every man may receive at least a moderate education, and thereby be enabled to read the histories of his own and other countries, by which he may duly appreciate the value of our free institutions, appears to be an object of vital importance, even on this account alone, to say nothing of the advantages and satisfaction to be derived from all being able to read the scriptures and other works, both of a religious and moral nature, for themselves.

— *Letter to the people of Sangamo County, March 9, 1832*

❧

I am slow to learn and slow to forget that which I have learned. My mind is like a piece of steel, very hard to scratch anything on it and almost impossible after you get it there to rub it out.

— *Remark to his friend Joshua Speed (n.d.[1])*

❧

A fool could learn about as well as a wise man, but after he had learned, it did not do him any good.

— *Remark to an acquaintance from Illinois (n.d.)*

❧

When the conduct of men is designed to be influenced, *persuasion*, kind, unassuming persuasion, should ever be adopted.

— *Speech to the Springfield Washingtonian Temperance Society, February 22, 1842*

❧

… what is the influence of fashion, but the influence that other people's actions have [on our own] actions, the strong inclination

---

[1] This abbreviation "n.d."—standing for "no date"—means I was not able to assign the *decade* (previous to 1860) or the *year* during the Civil War (1861–1865).

each of us feels to do as we see all our neighbors do? Nor is the influence of fashion confined to any particular thing or class of things. It is just as strong on one subject as another.

—Speech to the Springfield Washingtonian Temperance Society,
February 22, 1842

✻

How miserably things seem to be arranged in this world. If we have no friends, we have no pleasure; and if we have them, we are sure to lose them and be doubly pained by the loss.

—Letter to Joshua Speed, February 25, 1842

✻

The way for a young man to rise is to improve himself every way he can, never suspecting that anybody wishes to hinder him. Allow me to assure you that suspicion and jealousy never did help any man in any situation. There may sometimes be ungenerous attempts to keep a young man down; and they will succeed too, if he allows his mind to be diverted from its true channel to brood over the attempted injury. Cast about, and see if this feeling has not injured every person you have ever known to fall into it.

—Letter to William H. Herndon, Lincoln's law partner in Springfield,
Illinois, July 10, 1848

✻

This habit of uselessly wasting time is the whole difficulty; and it is vastly important to you, and still more so to your children that you should break this habit. It is more important to them, because they have longer to live and can keep out of an idle habit before they are in it; easier than they can get out after they are in.

—Letter to John D. Johnston, his stepbrother, December 24, 1848

✻

Resolve to be honest at all events; and if, in your own judgment, you can not be an honest lawyer, resolve to be honest without being a lawyer. Choose some other occupation.

—Notes for a lecture on law, July 1, 1850

I am from home too much of my time for a young man to read law
with me advantageously. If you are resolutely determined to make
a lawyer of yourself, the thing is more than half done already. It is
but a small matter whether you read *with* anybody or not. I did not
read with anyone. Get the books, and read and study them till you
understand them in their principal features; and that is the main
thing. It is of no consequence to be in a large town while you are
reading. I read at New Salem, which never had three hundred
people living in it. The *books*, and your *capacity* for understanding
them, are just the same in all places. ...

Always bear in mind that your own resolution to succeed is more
important than any other one thing.

—*Letter to Isham Reavis, November 5, 1855*

Free labor argues that as the Author of man makes every individual
with one head and one pair of hands, it was probably intended that
heads and hands should cooperate as friends, and that that particular head should direct and control that particular pair of hands. As
each man has one mouth to be fed and one pair of hands to furnish
food, it was probably intended that that particular pair of hands
should feed that particular mouth—that each head is the natural
guardian, director and protector of the hands and mouth insepara-
bly connected with it; and that being so, every head should be
cultivated and improved by whatever will add to its capacity for
performing its charge. In one word, free labor insists on universal
education.

—*Speech to the Wisconsin State Agricultural Society, Milwaukee,
Wisconsin, September 30, 1859*

It was a wild region, with many bears and other wild animals still
in the woods. There I grew up. There were some schools, so called;
but no qualification was ever required of a teacher, beyond "*readin,
writin, and cipherin,*" the rule of three. ... There was absolutely
nothing to excite ambition for education. Of course when I came
of age I did not know much. Still somehow, I could read, write,
and cipher to the rule of three, but that was all. I have not been
to school since. The little advance I now have upon this store of

education I have picked up from time to time under the pressure of necessity.

—*Letter to Jesse Fell, for an article in* Chester *(Pennsylvania)* County Times, *December 20, 1859*

ೋ

I remember how, when a mere child, I used to get irritated when anybody talked to me in a way I could not understand. I don't think I ever got angry at anything else in my life. ... I could not sleep, though I often tried to, when I got on such a hunt after an idea, until I had caught it; and when I thought I had got it, I was not satisfied until I had repeated it over and over, until I had put it in language plain enough, as I thought, for any boy I knew to comprehend. This was a kind of passion with me, and it has stuck by me; for I am never easy now, when I am handling a thought, till I have bounded it north, and bounded it south, and bounded it east, and bounded it west. ...

—*Conversation, with Reverend John Gulliver, March 9, 1860*

ೋ

Yours of the 24th asking "the best mode of obtaining a thorough knowledge of the law" is received. The mode is very simple, though laborious and tedious. It is only to get the books, and read, and study them carefully. ... Work, work, work, is the main thing.

—*Letter to John M. Brockman, September 25, 1860*

ೋ

Young gentlemen, excuse me for swearing before you; *by jings* is swearing, for my good old mother taught me that anything that had a *by* before it is swearing. I won't do so any more.

—*Remark to the men of the War Department's telegraph office, September 1861*

ೋ

Your good mother tells me you are feeling very badly in your new situation. Allow me to assure you it is a perfect certainty that you will, very soon, feel better—quite happy—if you only stick to the resolution you have taken to procure a military education. I am older than you, have felt badly myself, and *know* what I tell you is true. Adhere to your purpose and you will soon feel as well as you ever did. On the contrary, if you falter, and give up, you will lose the power of keeping any resolution, and will regret it all your life. Take the advice of a friend, who, though he never saw you, deeply sympathizes with you, and stick to your purpose.

—*Letter to Quintin Campbell, who had recently started at West Point; written at the request of Campbell's mother and Lincoln's wife, June 28, 1862*

❦

It is with deep grief that I learn of the death of your kind and brave father; and, especially, that it is affecting your young heart beyond what is common in such cases. In this sad world of ours, sorrow comes to all; and, to the young, it comes with bitterest agony, because it takes them unawares. The older have learned to ever expect it. I am anxious to afford some alleviation of your present distress. Perfect relief is not possible, except with time.

—*Letter to Fanny McCullough, December 23, 1862*

❦

The advice of a father to his son, "Beware of entrance to a quarrel, but being in, bear it that the opposed may beware of thee," is good, and yet not the best. Quarrel not at all. No man resolved to make the most of himself can spare time for personal contention. Still less can he afford to take all the consequences, including the vitiating of his temper and the loss of self-control. Yield larger things to which you can show no more than equal right; and yield lesser ones, though clearly your own. Better give your path to a dog than be bitten by him in contesting for the right. Even killing the dog would not cure the bite.

—*Letter to Captain James Cutts, October 26, 1863*

❦

Do good to those who hate you and turn their ill will to friendship.

—*Remark to his wife, Mary, when she "talked to him about former Secretary of the Treasury Salmon Chase and those who did him evil" (n.d.)*

FAITH, MORALITY, AND "GOD'S WILL"

The *preacher*, it is said, advocates temperance because he is a fanatic, and desires a union of the Church and State; the *lawyer*, from his pride and vanity of hearing himself speak; and the *hired agent*, for his salary. But when one who has long been known as a victim of intemperance bursts the fetters that have bound him, and appears before his neighbors "clothed, and in his right mind," a redeemed specimen of long lost humanity, and stands up with tears of joy trembling in eyes to tell of the miseries *once* endured, *now* to be endured no more forever; of his once naked and starving children now clad and fed comfortably; of a wife long weighed down with woe, weeping, and a broken heart, now restored to health, happiness and renewed affection; and how easily it all is done, once it is resolved to be done; however simple his language, there is a logic, and an eloquence in it, that few, with human feelings, can resist. They cannot say that *he* desires a union of church and state, for he is not a church member; they can not say *he* is vain of hearing himself speak, for his whole demeanor shows he would gladly avoid speaking at all; they cannot say *he* speaks for pay for he receives none, and asks for none. Nor can his sincerity in any way be doubted, or his sympathy for those he would persuade to imitate his example be denied.

—*Speech to the Springfield Washingtonian Temperance Society,*
February 22, 1842

❧

When the dram-seller and drinker were incessantly told, not in the accents of entreaty and persuasion, diffidently addressed by erring man to an erring brother, but in the thundering tones of anathema and denunciation with which the lordly Judge often groups together all the crimes of the felon's life and thrusts them in his face just ere he passes sentence of death upon him that *they* were the authors of all the vice and misery and crime in the land; that *they* were the manufacturers and material of all the thieves and robbers and murderers that infested the earth; that *their* houses were the workshops of the devil; and that *their persons* should be shunned by all the good and virtuous as moral pestilences—I say, when they were told all this, and in this way, it is not wonderful that they were slow, very slow, to acknowledge the truth of such denunciations, and to join the ranks of their denouncers in a hue and cry against themselves.

—*Speech to the Springfield Washingtonian Temperance Society,*
February 22, 1842

ა

In my judgment, such of us as have never fallen victims, have been spared more from the absence of appetite, than from any mental or moral superiority over those who have. Indeed, I believe, if we take habitual drunkards as a class, their heads and their hearts will bear an advantageous comparison with those of any other class. There seems ever to have been a proneness in the brilliant, and the warm-blooded, to fall into this vice. The demon of intemperance ever seems to have delighted in sucking the blood of genius and of generosity.

—*Speech to the Springfield Washingtonian Temperance Society,*
February 22, 1842

ა

That I am not a member of any Christian church is true; but I have never denied the truth of the Scriptures; and I have never spoken with intentional disrespect of religion in general, or of any denomination of Christians in particular.

... I do not think I could myself be brought to support a man for office whom I knew to be an open enemy of, and scoffer at, religion.

—*To the voters of the Seventh Congressional District on the charge that*
he was an "open scoffer" at religion, July 31, 1846

ა

I believe it is an established maxim in morals that he who makes an assertion without knowing whether it is true or false is guilty of falsehood; and the accidental truth of the assertion does not justify or excuse him.

—*Letter to the editor,* Illinois Gazette, *August 11, 1846*

There is a vague popular belief that lawyers are necessarily dishonest. I say vague, because when we consider to what extent confidence and honors are reposed in and conferred upon lawyers by the people, it appears improbable that their impression of dishonesty is very distinct and vivid. Yet the impression is common, almost universal.

—*Notes for a lecture on law, c. July 1850*

ઝ

Let us believe, as in the days of our youth, that [George] Washington was spotless; it makes human nature better to believe that one human being was perfect: that human perfection is possible.

—*Remark to an Illinois acquaintance, c. mid-1850s*

ઝ

A man cannot prove a negative, but he has a right to claim that when a man makes an affirmative charge, he must offer some proof to show the truth of what he says. I certainly cannot introduce testimony to show the negative about things, but I have a right to claim that if a man says he *knows* a thing, then he must show *how* he knows it. I always have a right to claim this, and it is not satisfactory to me that he may be "conscientious" on the subject.

—*First debate with Stephen Douglas, Ottawa, Illinois,*
August 21, 1858

ઝ

Constituted as man is, he has positive need of occasional recreation, and whatever can give him this, associated with virtue and advantage and free from vice and disadvantage, is a positive good.

—*Speech to the Wisconsin State Agricultural Society, Milwaukee,*
Wisconsin, September 30, 1859

ઝ

It is said an Eastern monarch once charged his wise men to invent him a sentiment to be ever in view, and which should be true and appropriate in all times and situations. They presented him the words, *"And this, too, shall pass away."* How much it expresses! How chastening in the hour of pride; how consoling in the depths of affliction! "And this, too, shall pass away." And yet, let us hope it is not *quite* true. Let us hope, rather, that by the best cultivation of the physical world, beneath and around us, and the intellectual and moral worlds within us, we shall secure an individual, social, and political prosperity and happiness whose course shall be onward and upward, and which, while the earth endures, shall not pass away.

—*Speech to the Wisconsin State Agricultural Society, Milwaukee, Wisconsin, September 30, 1859*

❦

Let us have faith that right makes might, and in that faith, let us, to the end, dare to do our duty as we understand it.

—*Speech, Cooper Union Institute, New York City, February 27, 1860*

❦

When one starts poor, as most do in the race of life, free society is such that he knows he can better his condition; he knows that there is no fixed condition of labor for his whole life. I am not ashamed to confess that twenty-five years ago I was a hired laborer, mauling rails, at work on a flatboat—just what might happen to any poor man's son! I want every man to have the chance—and I believe a black man is entitled to it—in which he *can* better his condition—when he may look forward and hope to be a hired laborer this year and the next, work for himself afterward, and finally to hire men to work for him.

—*Speech, New Haven, Connecticut, March 6, 1860*

❦

Here are twenty-three ministers of different denominations, and all of them are against me but three; and here are a great many prominent members of the churches, a very large majority of whom are against me. Mr. Bateman, I am not a Christian—God knows I would be one, but I have carefully read the Bible, and I do not so understand this book {drawing forth a pocket New Testament}. These men well know that I am for freedom in the territories, freedom everywhere as far as the Constitution and laws will permit, and that my opponents are for slavery. They know this and yet, with this book in their hands, in the light of which human bondage cannot live a moment, they are going to vote against me. I do not understand it at all.

—Remark to Illinois superintendent of public instruction, Newton Bateman, late October 1860

ço

The fact is, I don't like to hear cut and dried sermons. No—when I hear a man preach, I like to see him act as if he were fighting bees!

—Remark to the sculptor Leonard Wells Volk, c. 1860

ço

Do you believe any man ever lived who had responsibilities laid upon him and saw great difficulties before him he could not see his way out of who did not look to some wiser and stronger being for help and wisdom to support and guide him? That is my condition.

—Remark to an Illinois lawyer, before leaving for Washington, February 1861

ço

A simple faith in God is good enough for me, and beyond that I do not concern myself very much.

—Remark to the pastor Phineas D. Gurley, after the death of Lincoln's son Willie in February 1862

ço

The will of God prevails. In great contests each party claims to act in accordance with the will of God. Both *may* be, and one *must* be, wrong. God cannot be *for* and *against* the same thing at the same time. In the present civil war it is quite possible that God's purpose is something different from the purpose of either party—and yet the human instrumentalities, working just as they do, are of the best adaptation to effect His purpose.

> —*"Meditation on the Divine Will," c. September 2, 1862*

ꝏ

I am almost ready to say ... that God wills this contest, and wills that it shall not end yet.

> —*"Meditation on the Divine Will," c. September 2, 1862*

ꝏ

If I had had my way, this war would never have been commenced; if I had been allowed my way this war would have ended before this, but we find it still continues; and we must believe that He permits it for some wise purpose of his own, mysterious and unknown to us; and though with our limited understandings we may not be able to comprehend it, yet we cannot but believe that he who made the world still governs it.

> —*Letter to Eliza Gurney, October 26, 1862*

ꝏ

Since your last annual assembling another year of health and bountiful harvests has passed. And while it has not pleased the Almighty to bless us with a return of peace, we can but press on, guided by the best light He gives us, trusting that in His own good time and wise way all will yet be well.

> —*Annual Message to Congress, December 1, 1862*

ꝏ

It is most cheering and encouraging for me to know that in the efforts which I have made and am making for the restoration of a righteous peace to our country, I am upheld and sustained by the good wishes and prayers of God's people. No one is more deeply than myself aware that without His favor our highest wisdom is but as foolishness and that our most strenuous efforts would avail nothing in the shadow of His displeasure. I am conscious of no desire for my country's welfare that is not in consonance with His will, and of no plan upon which we may not ask His blessing. It seems to me that if there be one subject upon which all good men may unitedly agree, it is imploring the gracious favor of the God of Nations upon the struggles our people are making for the preservation of their precious birthright of civil and religious liberty.

—Letter to Caleb Russell and Sallie Fenton of the Religious Society of Friends, Iowa, January 5, 1863

 familiar

I have often wished that I was a more devout man than I am.

—Remarks to the Presbyterian Synod of Baltimore, October 24, 1863

familiar

On principle I dislike an oath which requires a man to swear he *has* not done wrong. It rejects the Christian principle of forgiveness on terms of repentance. I think it is enough if the man does no wrong *hereafter*.

—Letter to Secretary of War Edwin Stanton, February 5, 1864

familiar

I claim not to have controlled events, but confess plainly that events have controlled me. ... If God now wills the removal of a great wrong, and wills also that we of the North as well as you of the South shall pay fairly for our complicity in that wrong, impartial history will find therein new cause to attest and revere the justice and goodness of God.

—Letter to Albert G. Hodges, April 4, 1864

familiar

When, a year or two ago, those professedly holy men of the South met in the semblance of prayer and devotion, and, in the name of Him who said, "As ye would all men should do unto you, do ye even so unto them," appealed to the Christian world to aid them in doing to a whole race of men as they would have no man do unto themselves, to my thinking, they condemned and insulted

God and His church far more than did Satan when he tempted the
Savior with the Kingdoms of the earth. The devil's attempt was no
more false and far less hypocritical. But let me forbear, remember-
ing it is also written, "Judge not, lest ye be judged."

> —*Letter to the Reverend George B. Ide, J. R. Doolittle and*
> *A. Hubbell, May 30, 1864*

❧

The purposes of the Almighty are perfect, and must prevail, though
we erring mortals may fail to accurately perceive them in advance.
We hoped for a happy termination of this terrible war long before
this, but God knows best, and has ruled otherwise. ... we must
work earnestly in the best light He gives us, trusting that so working still conduces to the great ends He ordains. Surely He intends
some great good to follow this mighty convulsion, which no mortal could make, and no mortal could stay.

> —*Letter to Eliza Gurney, September 4, 1864*

❧

... I, Abraham Lincoln, President of the United States, do hereby
appoint and set apart the last Thursday in November next as a day
which I desire to be observed by all my fellow citizens wherever
they may then be as a day of Thanksgiving and Praise to Almighty
God the beneficent Creator and Ruler of the Universe. And I do
farther recommend to my fellow citizens aforesaid that on that occasion they do reverently humble themselves in the dust and from
thence offer up penitent and fervent prayers and supplications to
the Great Disposer of events for a turn of the inestimable blessings
of Peace, Union and Harmony throughout the land, which it has
pleased him to assign as a dwelling place for ourselves and for our
posterity throughout all generations.

> —*Thanksgiving proclamation, October 20, 1864*

❧

... [immigrants are] one of the principal replenishing streams which
are appointed by Providence to repair the ravages of internal war
and its wastes of national strength and health.

> —*Annual message, December 6, 1864*

You say your husband is a religious man; tell him when you meet him that I say I am not much of a judge of religion, but that, in my opinion, the religion that sets men to rebel and fight against their government, because, as they think, that government does not sufficiently help *some* men to eat their bread on the sweat of *other* men's faces, is not the sort of religion upon which people can get to heaven.

—*Remarks to two women from Tennessee asking for the release of their rebel husbands as prisoners of war, December 6, 1864*

❧

Fondly do we hope—fervently do we pray—that this mighty scourge of war may speedily pass away. Yet, if God wills that it continue until all the wealth piled by the bondman's two hundred and fifty years of unrequited toil shall be sunk, and until every drop of blood drawn with the lash shall be paid by another drawn with the sword, as was said three thousand years ago, so still it must be said: The judgments of the Lord are true, and righteous altogether.

—*Letter to Amanda Hall, March 20, 1865*

❧

FATHERS AND SONS

Say to him that if we could meet now, it is doubtful whether it would not be more painful than pleasant; but that if it be his lot to go now, he will soon have a joyous meeting with many loved ones gone before; and where the rest of us, through the help of God, hope ere long to join them.

—*Letter to John D. Johnston, his stepbrother, on Lincoln's father's illness, January 12, 1851*

❧

It is my pleasure that my children are free, happy, and unrestrained by parental tyranny. Love is the chain to lock a child to its parent.

—*A remark he often made, according to his wife Mary, whenever he was "chided or praised" for his indulgence of his children (n.d.)*

Well, Nicolay, my boy is gone—he is actually gone!
> —*Remark to his secretary John Nicolay, on the death from disease of Lincoln's son Willie, February 20, 1862*

∾

My poor boy, he was too good for this earth. God has called him home. I know he is much better off in heaven, but then we loved him so. It is hard, hard to have him die!
> —*Remark on his son Willie's death, February 20, 1862*

∾

Did you ever dream of some lost friend and feel that you were having a sweet communion with him, and yet have a consciousness that it was not a reality? … That is the way I dream of my lost boy Willie.
> —*Remark to Colonel Le Grand Cannon on William Wallace "Willie" Lincoln, who died at age eleven in February of 1862*

∾

Think you better put Tad's pistol away. I had an ugly dream about him.
> —*Telegram to his wife, about their son Tad, June 9, 1863*

∾

Let him run; there's time enough yet for him to learn his letters and get pokey. Bob was just such a little rascal, and now he is a very decent boy.
> —*Remark to journalist and friend Noah Brooks on Robert and Tad Lincoln (n.d.)*

∾

HIS OWN LIFE AND CHARACTER

> Abraham Lincoln
> his hand and pen
> he will be good but
> god knows when
>
> —*Verses in his boyhood sum book,*
> *c. 1824–1826*

ॐ

Every man is said to have his peculiar ambition. Whether it be true or not, I can say for one that I have no other so great as that of being truly esteemed of my fellow men by rendering myself worthy of their esteem.

> —*Letter to the people of Sangamo County, March 9, 1832*

ॐ

As to fees, it is impossible to establish a rule that will apply in all, or even a great many cases. We believe we are never accused of being very unreasonable in this particular; and we would always be easily satisfied, provided we could see the money—but whatever fees we earn at a distance, if not paid before, we have noticed we never hear of after the work is done. We therefore are growing a little sensitive on that point.

> —*Letter to a prospective out-of-town legal client, November 2, 1842*

ॐ

Being elected to Congress, though I am very grateful to our friends for having done it, has not pleased me as much as I expected.

> —*Letter to Joshua Speed, October 22, 1846*

ॐ

By the way, Mr. Speaker, did you know I am a military hero? Yes, sir, in the days of the Black Hawk war [1832], I fought, bled, and came away. Speaking of General Cass's career reminds me of my own. I was not at Stillman's defeat, but I was about as near it as Cass was to Hull's surrender; and, like him, I saw the place very soon afterwards. It is quite certain I did not break my sword, for I had none to break; but I bent a musket pretty badly on one occasion. If Cass broke his sword, the idea is, he broke it in desperation; I bent the musket by accident. If General Cass went in advance of me in picking whortleberries, I guess I surpassed him in charges upon the wild onions. If he saw any live fighting Indians, it was more than I did, but I had a good many bloody struggles with the mosquitoes; and although I never fainted from loss of blood, I can truly say I was often very hungry.

—*Speech in the U.S. House of Representatives, July 27, 1848*

Your note, requesting my "signature with a sentiment," was received and should have been answered long since, but that it was mislaid. I am not a very sentimental man; and the best sentiment I can think of is, that if you collect the signatures of all persons who are no less distinguished than I, you will have a very undistinguishing mass of names.

—*Letter to C. U. Schlater, January 5, 1849*

I can remember our life in Kentucky: the cabin, the stinted living, the sale of our possessions, and the journey with my father and mother to southern Indiana. It was pretty pinching times at first in Indiana, getting the cabin built and the clearing for the crops, but presently we got reasonably comfortable, and my father married again. ... My father had suffered greatly for want of an education, and he determined at an early day that I should be well educated. And what do you think he said his ideas of a good education were? We had an old dog-eared arithmetic in our house, and father determined that somehow, or somehow else, I should cipher through that book.

—*Remark to Illinois lawyer Leonard Swett, Fall 1853*

Hadn't we better withdraw that plea? You know it's a sham, and a sham is very often but another name for a lie. Don't let it go on

record. The cursed thing may come staring us in the face long after
this suit has been forgotten.

—*Remark to William H. Herndon, Lincoln's law partner in*
Springfield, Illinois (n.d.)

ം

Men are greedy to publish the successes of efforts, but meanly shy
as to publishing the failures of man. Many men are ruined by this
one-sided practice of concealment of blunders and failures.

—*Remark to William H. Herndon, Lincoln's law partner in*
Springfield, Illinois, mid-1850s

ം

... when a man hears himself misrepresented just a little, why, it
rather provokes him, at least so I find it with me; but when he
finds the misrepresentation very gross, why it sometimes amuses
him.

—*Debate reply to Stephen Douglas, Ottawa, Illinois,*
August 21, 1858

ം

I was not much accustomed to flattery. I was very much like the
hoosier with the gingerbread—he said that he loved it better and
got less of it than any other man.

—*Debate reply to Stephen Douglas, Ottawa, Illinois,*
August 21, 1858

ം

I don't state a thing and say I know when I don't.

—*Debate reply to Stephen Douglas, Jonesboro, Illinois,*
September 15, 1858

ം

I don't want to be subject to the imputation of illiberality of dealing
with an adversary. I would despise myself if I supposed that either

in a court or a political discussion I was capable of dealing with less liberality than I was receiving.

—*Debate with Stephen Douglas, rejoinder, Charleston, Illinois,*
September 18, 1858

❧

I have to trust to a reading community to judge whether I advance just views, or whether I state views that are revolutionary or hypocritical. I believe myself guilty of no such thing as the latter; and of course I cannot claim that I am entirely free from error in the views and principles that I advance.

—*Debate with Stephen Douglas, reply, Galesburg, Illinois,*
October 7, 1858

❧

He did not misstate, in one of his early speeches, when he called me an amiable man, though, perhaps, he did when he called me an intelligent man.

—*Debate with Stephen Douglas, opening speech, Quincy, Illinois,*
October 13, 1858

❧

I agree that there is selfishness enough among office seekers. We are desperately selfish, I believe the Bible says, somewhere, and I believe that I should have discovered that fact if the Bible had not said it. I am not less selfish than other men, but I do claim that I am not more selfish than is Judge Douglas.

—*Debate with Stephen Douglas, reply, Alton, Illinois, October 15, 1858*

❧

I am glad I made the late race. It gave me a hearing on the great and durable question of the age, which I could have had in no other way; and though I now sink out of view, and shall be forgotten, I believe I have made some marks which will tell for the cause of civil liberty long after I am gone.

—*Letter to Anson Henry, November 19, 1858*

I expect the result of the election went hard with you. So it did with me, too, perhaps not quite so hard as you may have supposed. I have an abiding faith that we shall beat them in the long run. Step by step the objects of the leaders will become too plain for the people to stand them. I write merely to let you know that I am neither dead nor dying.

—Letter to Alexander Sympson, December 12, 1858

❧

Herewith is a little sketch [of autobiography], as you requested. There is not much of it, for the reason, I suppose, that there is not much of me.

—Letter to Jesse Fell, for an article in Chester *(Pennsylvania)* County Times, *December 20, 1859*

❧

If any personal description of me is thought desirable, it may be said I am, in height, six feet, four inches, nearly; lean in flesh, weighing, on average, one hundred and eighty pounds; dark complexion, with coarse black hair, and gray eyes—no other marks or brands recollected.

—Letter to Jesse Fell, for an article in Chester *(Pennsylvania)* County Times, *December 20, 1859*

❧

My dear little Miss,

Your very agreeable letter of the 15th is received.

I regret the necessity of saying I have no daughters. I have three sons—one seventeen, one nine, and one seven years of age. They, with their mother, constitute my whole family.

As to the whiskers, having never worn any, do you not think people would call it a piece of silly affectation if I were to begin it now?

—Letter to Grace Bedell, eleven years old, who suggested he grow a beard, October 19, 1860

Give our clients to understand that the election of a president makes no change in the firm of Lincoln and Herndon. If I live, I'm coming back sometime, and then we'll go right on practicing law as if nothing had ever happened.

> —*Remark to William H. Herndon, Lincoln's law partner in Springfield, Illinois, February 1861*

❧

Here I have lived a quarter of a century, and have passed from a young to an old man. Here my children have been born, and one is buried. I now leave, not knowing when or whether ever I may return, with a task before me greater than that which rested upon Washington. Without the assistance of that Divine Being who ever attended him, I cannot succeed. With that assistance, I cannot fail.

> —*Speech, on leaving Springfield, Illinois, by train for Washington, D.C., February 11, 1861*

❧

I once heard you say in a lecture that a Kentuckian seems to say by his air and manners, "Here am I; if you don't like me, the worse for you."

> —*Remark to the poet Ralph Waldo Emerson, February 1862*

❧

I recollect once being outside a stage in Illinois, and a man sitting by me offered me a cigar. I told him I had no vices. He said nothing, smoked for some time, and then grunted out, "It's my experience that folks who have no vices have plaguy few virtues."

> —*Remark to an English journalist, 1862*

❧

If I have one vice, and I can call it nothing else, it is not to be able to say no! Thank God for not making me a woman, but if He had, I suppose He would have made me just as ugly as He did, and no one would ever have tempted me.

> —*Remark to Egbert Viele, May 1862*

Well, now, I never thought M. had anything more than average abilities, when we were young men together—and he wants to be superintendent of the mint! ... But, then, I suppose he thought the same thing about me, and—here I am!

—Remark to journalist and friend Noah Brooks (n.d.)

જી

I long ago made up my mind that if anybody wants to kill me, he will do it. If I wore a shirt of mail and kept myself surrounded by a bodyguard, it would be all the same. There are a thousand ways of getting at a man if it is desirable that he should be killed. Besides, in this case, it seems to me, the man who would come after me would be just as objectionable to my enemies.

—Remark to journalist and friend Noah Brooks,
c. Spring 1863

જી

Mother has got a notion into her head that I shall be assassinated, and to please her I take a cane when I go over to the War Department at nights—when I don't forget it.

—Remark on his wife Mary's concern, to Noah Brooks,
c. Spring 1863

જી

With all the fearful strain that is upon me night and day, if I did not laugh I should die.

—Remark to a cabinet minister who wondered why Lincoln was reading
a book of humor (n.d.)

જી

I have endured a great deal of ridicule without much malice; and have received a great deal of kindness, not quite free from ridicule. I am used to it.

—Letter to the actor James H. Hackett, November 2, 1863

Common looking people are the best in the world; that is the reason the Lord makes so many of them.

> —*Recounting, to his assistant private secretary John Hay, a remark made in his dream, December 23, 1863*

❧

It is impossible to get my graceful motions in—that's the reason why none of the pictures are like me.

> —*Remark to a newspaper reporter on why his portraits hadn't successfully caught him*

❧

I was once accosted ... by a stranger, who said, "Excuse me, sir, but I have an article in my possession which belongs to you." "How is that?" I asked, considerably astonished. The stranger took a jackknife from his pocket. "This knife," said he, "was placed in my hands some years ago with the injunction that I was to keep it until I found a man uglier than myself. I have carried it from that time to this. Allow me to say, sir, that I think you are fairly entitled to the property."

> —*Anecdote about the period when Lincoln practiced law on the Illinois State circuit, told to his portrait painter, Francis B. Carpenter, 1864*

❧

It is very strange that I, a boy brought up in the woods, and seeing, as it were, but little of the world, should be drifted into the very apex of this great event.

> —*Remark to Josiah Blackburn, c. late July 1864*

❧

It is a little singular that I, who am not a vindictive man, should have always been before the people for election in canvases marked for their bitterness, always but once: When I came to Congress it was a quiet time. But always besides that the contests in which I have been prominent have been marked with great rancor.

> —*Remark to his assistant private secretary John Hay on election day, November 8, 1864*

If any man ceases to attack me, I never remember the past against him.

—Remark to his assistant private secretary John Hay,
November 1864

ക

I cannot bring myself to believe that any human being lives who would do me any harm.

—Remark about a reported threat on his life on the day he arrived in
Richmond, Virginia, April 4, 1865

ക

Creswell, old fellow, everything is bright this morning. The war is over. It has been a tough time, but we have lived it out. Or some of us have.

—In conversation to Senator John Creswell of Maryland,
April 14, 1865

ക

We must both be more cheerful in the future. Between the war and the loss of our darling Willie, we have both been very miserable.

—Remark to his wife Mary, April 14, 1865. (One of their sons had
died of disease in 1862. On this night the Lincolns went to the theater,
and the President was shot.)

ക

LAW AND THE CONSTITUTION

When men take it in their heads today to hang gamblers or burn murderers, they should recollect that, in the confusion usually attending such transactions, they will be as likely to hang or burn someone who is neither a gambler nor a murderer as one who is; and that, acting upon the example they set, the mob of tomorrow

may, and probably will, hang or burn some of them by the very
same mistake.

— *"The Perpetuation of Our Political Institutions": Address before the
Young Men's Lyceum of Springfield, Illinois, January 27, 1838*

... by the operation of the mobocratic spirit, which all must admit
is now abroad in the land, the strongest bulwark of any Government,
and particularly of those constituted like ours, may effectually be
broken down and destroyed—I mean the *attachment* of the People.
... whenever the vicious portion of population shall be permitted
to gather in bands of hundreds and thousands, and burn churches,
ravage and rob provision-stores, throw printing presses into rivers,
shoot editors, and hang and burn obnoxious persons at pleasure,
and with impunity; depend on it, this Government cannot last.

— *"The Perpetuation of Our Political Institutions": Address before the
Young Men's Lyceum of Springfield, Illinois, January 27, 1838*

As the patriots of '76 did to the support of the Constitution and
laws, let every American pledge his life, his property, and his sacred
honor; let every man remember that to violate the law is to trample
on the blood of his father and to tear the character of his own and
his children's liberty.

— *"The Perpetuation of Our Political Institutions": Address before the
Young Men's Lyceum of Springfield, Illinois, January 27, 1838*

How effectual have penitentiaries heretofore been in preventing
the crimes they were established to suppress? Has not confinement
in them long been the legal penalty of larceny, forgery, robbery,
and many other crimes, in almost all the states? And yet, are not
those crimes committed weekly, daily, nay, and even hourly in
every one of those states? Again, the gallows has long been the
penalty of murder, and yet we scarcely open a newspaper that does
not relate a new case of crime. If, then, the penitentiary has *heretofore* failed to prevent larceny, forgery and robbery, and the gallows

and halter have likewise failed to prevent murder, by what process of reasoning, I ask, is it that we are to conclude the penitentiary will hereafter prevent the stealing of the public money?
—*Speech, Hall of the House of Representatives, Springfield, Illinois, December 26, 1839*

ॐ

You say A. is white, and B. is black. It is *color*, then; the lighter having the right to enslave the darker? Take care. By this rule, you are to be slave to the first man you meet with a fairer skin than your own.
—*Notes, c. July 1846*

ॐ

Law is nothing else but the best reason of wise men applied for ages to the transactions and business of mankind.
—*Remark to William H. Herndon, Lincoln's law partner in Springfield, Illinois (n.d.)*

ॐ

... if all men were just, there still would be *some*, though not *so much*, need of government.
—*Note for a lecture, c. July 1, 1854*

ॐ

The legitimate object of government is to do for a community of people whatever they need to have done, but cannot do, *at all*, or cannot, *so well do*, for themselves—in their separate and individual capacities. In all that the people can individually do as well for themselves, government ought not to interfere.
—*Note for a lecture, c. July 1, 1854*

ॐ

You can better succeed with the ballot. You can peaceably then redeem the government and preserve the liberties of mankind through your votes and voice and moral influence. ... Let there be peace. Revolutionize through the ballot box and restore the government once more to the affections and hearts of men by making it express, as it was intended to do, the highest spirit of justice and liberty.

—*Speech to Springfield abolitionists, c. 1855*

ى

In your assumption that there may be a fair decision of the slavery question in Kansas, I plainly see you and I would differ about the Nebraska law. I look upon that enactment not as a *law*, but as *violence* from the beginning. It was conceived in violence, passed in violence, is maintained in violence, and is being executed in violence. I say it was conceived in violence, because the destruction of the Missouri Compromise, under the circumstances, was nothing less than violence. It was passed in violence, because it could not have passed at all but for the votes of many members, in violent disregard of the known will of their constituents. It is maintained in violence because the elections since clearly demand its repeal, and this demand is openly disregarded.

—*Letter to Joshua Speed, August 24, 1855*

ى

All the powers of earth seem rapidly combining against him. ... They have him in his prison house; they have searched his person, and left no prying instrument with him. One after another they have closed the heavy iron doors upon him, and now they have him, as it were, bolted in with a lock of a hundred keys, which can never be unlocked without the concurrence of every key; the keys in the hands of a hundred different men, and they scattered to a hundred different and distant places, and they stand musing as to what invention, in all the dominions of mind and matter, can be produced to make the impossibility of his escape more complete than it is.

—*Speech on the Dred Scott Decision, Springfield, Illinois,*
June 26, 1857

I am for the people of the whole nation doing just as they please in all matters which concern the whole nation; for those of each part doing just as they choose in all matters which concern no other part; and for each individual doing just as he chooses in all matters which concern nobody else. This is the principle. Of course I am content with any exception which the Constitution or the actually existing state of things makes a necessity. But neither the principle nor the exception will admit the indefinite spread and perpetuity of human slavery.

—*Draft of a speech, c. May 18, 1858*

❧

With public sentiment, nothing can fail; without it, nothing can succeed. Consequently, he who molds public sentiment goes deeper than he who enacts statutes or pronounces decisions. He makes statutes and decisions possible or impossible to be executed.
—*First debate with Stephen Douglas, Ottawa, Illinois,*
August 21, 1858

❧

What is Popular Sovereignty? Is it the right of the people to have slavery or not have it, as they see fit, in the territories? I will state—and I have an able man to watch me—my understanding is that Popular Sovereignty, as now applied to the question of slavery, does allow the people of a Territory to have slavery if they want to, but does not allow them *not* to have it if they *do not* want it.

—*First debate with Stephen Douglas, Ottawa, Illinois,*
August 21, 1858

❧

I have asked the attention of the Judge to the fact that he once opposed the Supreme Court of this State, his opposition ending in the curious fact of his sitting down on the bench—he getting his name of Judge in that very way. I can get no answer from the Judge on all this. I can get that far in the canvas and no further. All I can get from him is that all of us who stand by the decision of the Supreme Court are the friends of the Constitution and all you fellows that dare question it in any way are enemies of the Constitution. Now, in this very devoted position, in opposition to all the great political leaders that he has held as great political leaders—now, in this adherence there is something very marked, and there is something very marked in his adherence to it—not adhering to it on its merits, for he does not discuss it at all, but as being obligatory upon every one because of the source whence it comes, as that which no man may gainsay, is another marked feature of it. It marks it in this respect, that it commits him to the next one as firmly as it does to this.

—*Debate with Stephen Douglas, reply, Galesburg, Illinois,*
October 7, 1858

ॐ

... the institution of slavery is only mentioned in the Constitution of the United States two or three times, and in neither of these cases does the word "slavery" or "negro" occur; but covert language is used each time, and for a purpose full of significance. ... and that purpose was that in our Constitution, which it was hoped and is still hoped will endure forever—when it should be read by intelligent and patriotic men, after the institution of slavery had passed from among us—there should be nothing on the face of the great charter of liberty suggesting that such a thing as negro slavery had ever existed among us.

—*Seventh debate with Stephen Douglas, Alton, Illinois,*
October 15, 1858

ॐ

It is not true that our fathers, as Judge Douglas assumes, made this government part slave and part free. Understand the sense in which he puts it. He assumes that slavery is a rightful thing within itself—was introduced by the framers of the Constitution. The exact truth is that they found the institution existing among us, and they left it as they found it. But in making the government they left this institution with many clear marks of disapprobation upon it. They found slavery among them and they left it among them because of the difficulty—the absolute impossibility of its immediate removal.

—Seventh debate with Stephen Douglas, Alton, Illinois,
October 15, 1858

๛

I ask you to consider well if we have any difficulty or quarrel among ourselves about the cranberry laws of Indiana, or the oyster laws of Virginia, or about the timber laws of Maine and New Hampshire, or about the fact that Louisiana produces sugar and we produce flour and not sugar. When have we had quarrels about these things? Never no such thing. On the other hand, when have we had perfect peace in regard to this thing, which I say is an element of discord in this nation? We have sometimes had peace, and when was that? We have had peace whenever the institution of slavery remained quiet where it was, and we have had turmoil and difficulty whenever it has made a struggle to spread out where it was not. I ask, then, if experience does not teach, if it does not speak in thunder tones, that that policy that gives peace being returned to, gives promise of peace again.

—Debate with Stephen Douglas, reply, Alton, Illinois,
October 15, 1858

๛

To correct the evils, great and small, which spring from want of sympathy and from positive enmity among *strangers*, as nations or as individuals, is one of the highest functions of civilization.

—Speech to the Wisconsin State Agricultural Society, Milwaukee,
Wisconsin, September 30, 1859

๛

I dare not trust this case on presumptions that this court knows all things. I argued the case on the presumption that the court did not know any thing.

—Remark to William H. Herndon (n.d.)

I suppose you will never forget that trial down in Montgomery County, where the lawyer associated with you gave away the whole case in his opening speech. I saw you signaling to him, but you couldn't stop him. Now, that's just the way with me and [President] Buchanan. He is giving away the case, and I have nothing to say and can't stop him.

—*Remark to his friend and fellow Illinois lawyer Joseph Gillespie, late 1860*

ॐ

May I beg of you to consider the difficulties of my position and solicit your kind assistance in it? Our security in the seizing of arms for our destruction will amount to nothing at all if we are never to make mistakes in searching a place where there are none. I shall continue to do the very best I can to discriminate between *true* and *false* men. In the mean time, let me, once more, beg your assistance in allaying irritations which are unavoidable.

—*Letter to "unidentified persons," c. September 15, 1861*

ॐ

The traitor against the general government forfeits his slave, at least as justly as he does any other property; and he forfeits both to the government against which he offends. The government, so far as there can be ownership, thus owns the forfeited slaves; and the question for Congress, in regard to them, is, "Shall they be made free, or be sold to new masters?" I perceive no objection to Congress deciding in advance that they shall be free.

—*Message to the 37th Congress, Second Session, July 17, 1862*

ॐ

Long experience has shown that armies cannot be maintained unless desertion shall be punished by the severe penalty of death. The case requires, and the law and the Constitution sanction, this punishment. Must I shoot a simple-minded soldier boy who deserts while I must not touch a hair of a wily agitator who induces him to desert? This is none the less injurious when effected by getting a father, or brother, or friend into a public meeting, and there working upon his feelings till he is persuaded to write the soldier boy that he is fighting in a bad cause, for a wicked administration of a contemptible government, too weak to arrest and punish him if he shall desert. I think that in such a case to silence the agitator and save the boy is not only constitutional, but, withal, a great mercy.

—Letter to Erastus Corning and others on the arrest of the "Copperhead" Clement L. Vallandigham, June 12, 1863

∽

… the Constitution is not in its application in all respects the same in cases of rebellion or invasion involving the public safety as it is in times of profound peace and public security. The Constitution itself makes the distinction, and I can no more be persuaded that the government can constitutionally take no strong measures in time of rebellion, because it can be shown that the same could not be lawfully taken in time of peace, than I can be persuaded that a particular drug is not good medicine for a sick man because it can be shown to not be good food for a well one.

—Letter to Erastus Corning and others on the arrest of the "Copperhead" Clement L. Vallandigham, June 12, 1863

∽

Was it possible to lose the nation, and yet preserve the Constitution? By general law, life and limb must be protected; yet often a limb must be amputated to save a life; but a life is never wisely given to save a limb. I felt that measures, otherwise unconstitutional, might become lawful by becoming indispensable to the preservation of the Constitution through the preservation of the nation. Right or wrong, I assumed this ground, and now avow it. I could not feel that, to the best of my ability, I had even tried to preserve the Constitution if, to save slavery, or any minor matter, I should permit the wreck of government, country, and Constitution all together.

—Remarks to Kentucky governor Thomas Bramlette, Frankfort Commonwealth editor Albert Hodges, and Senator Archibald Dixon, March 26, 1864

Judge —— held the strongest ideas of rigid government and close construction that I ever met. It was said of him, on one occasion, that he would hang a man for blowing his nose in the street, but he would quash the indictment if it failed to specify which hand he blew it with.

—*Remark to his portrait painter, Francis B. Carpenter,*
Spring 1864

෮

The pilots on our Western rivers steer from *point to point* as they call it—setting the course of the boat no farther than they can see; and that is all I propose to myself in this great problem.

—*Remark to Maine editor James G. Blaine, on his*
reconstruction policy (c. 1864)

෮

Neither slavery nor involuntary servitude, except as a punishment for crime whereof the party shall have been duly convicted, shall exist within the United States, or any place subject to their jurisdiction.

—*Submission of "a proposition to amend the Constitution of the United States," the 13th Amendment, February 1, 1865*

෮

POLITICS

My case is thrown exclusively upon the independent voters of this county, and if elected they will have conferred a favor upon me, for which I shall be unremitting in my labors to compensate. But if the good people in their wisdom shall see fit to keep me in the background, I have been too familiar with disappointments to be very much chagrined.

—*Communication to the People of Sangamo County,*
March 9, 1832

My politics are short and sweet, like the old woman's dance.
>—*Speech while campaigning for the Illinois Legislature,*
>*in Pappsville, 1832*

❧

These capitalists generally act harmoniously and in concert to fleece the people, and now that they have got into a quarrel with themselves, we are called upon to appropriate the people's money to settle the quarrel.
>—*Speech in the Illinois Legislature, January 11, 1837*

❧

Mr. Chairman, this work is exclusively the work of politicians, a set of men who have interests aside from the interests of the people, and who, to say the most of them, are, taken as a mass, at least one long step removed from honest men. I say this with the greater freedom, because, being a politician myself, none can regard it as personal.
>—*Speech in the Illinois Legislature, January 11, 1837*

❧

The *probability* that we may fall in the struggle ought not to deter us from the support of a cause we believe to be just; it *shall not* deter me. If ever I feel the soul within me elevate and expand to those dimensions not wholly unworthy of its Almighty Architect, it is when I contemplate the cause of my country deserted by all the world beside, and I standing up boldly and alone and hurling defiance at her victorious oppressors. Here, without contemplating consequences, before High Heaven, and in the face of the world, I swear eternal fidelity to the just cause, as I deem it, of the land of my life, my liberty and my love. And who, that thinks with me, will not fearlessly adopt the oath that I take? Let none falter who thinks he is right, and we may succeed. But if, after all, we shall fail, be it so. We still shall have the proud consolation of saying to our consciences, and to the departed shade of our country's freedom, that the cause approved of our judgment, and adored of our hearts, in disaster, in chains, in torture, in death, we *never* faltered in defending.

—*Speech, Hall of the House of Representatives, Springfield, Illinois,*
December 26, 1839

ॐ

"We are not to do *evil* that good may come." This general proposition is doubtless correct; but did it apply? If by your votes you could have prevented the *extension, etc.,* of slavery, would it not have been *good* and not *evil* so to have used your votes, even though it involved the casting of them for a slave-holder? By the *fruit* the tree is to be known. An *evil* tree can not bring forth *good* fruit. If the fruit of electing Mr. Clay would have been to prevent the extension of slavery, could the act of electing have been *evil?*

—*Letter to Williamson Durley, an abolitionist, October 3, 1845*

ॐ

It is certain that struggles between candidates do not strengthen a party; but who are most responsible for these struggles, those who are willing to live and let live, or those who are resolved, at all hazards, to take care of "number one"?

—*Letter to John Hardin, February 7, 1846*

ॐ

When the war began, it was my opinion that all those who, because of knowing too little, or because of knowing too much, could not conscientiously approve the conduct of the President (in the beginning of it), should, nevertheless, as good citizens and patriots remain silent on that point, at least till the war should be ended.

—*Speech on the war with Mexico, U.S. House of Representatives,*
January 12, 1848

ॐ

... I more than suspect already that he [President James K. Polk] is deeply conscious of being in the wrong; that he feels the blood of this war, like the blood of Abel, is crying to Heaven against him; that he ordered General Taylor into the midst of a peaceful

Mexican settlement, purposely to bring on a war; that originally having some strong motive—what I will not stop now to give my opinion concerning—to involve the two countries in a war, and trusting to escape scrutiny by fixing the public gaze upon the exceeding brightness of military glory—that attractive rainbow that rises in showers of blood—that serpent's eye that charms to destroy—he plunged into it, and has swept *on* and *on*, till, disappointed in his calculation of the ease with which Mexico might be subdued, he now finds himself he knows not where.

—*Speech to the U.S. House of Representatives on the Mexican War, January 12, 1848*

ج

… it is a singular omission in this message that it nowhere intimates *when* the President expects the war to terminate. At its beginning, General Scott was, by this same President, driven into disfavor, if not disgrace, for intimating that peace could not be conquered in less than three or four months. But now, at the end of about twenty months, during which time our arms have given us the most splendid successes—every department, and every part, land and water, officers and privates, regulars and volunteers, doing all that men *could* do, and hundreds of things which it had ever before been thought men could *not* do—after all this, this same President gives us a long message without showing us that, *as to the end*, he himself has even an imaginary conception. As I have before said, he knows not where he is. He is a bewildered, confounded, and miserably perplexed man. God grant he may be able to show there is not something about his conscience more painful than all his mental perplexity!

—*Speech to the U.S. House of Representatives on the Mexican War, January 12, 1848*

ج

Allow the President to invade a neighboring nation whenever *he* shall deem it necessary to repel an invasion, and you allow him to do so *whenever he may choose to say* he deems it necessary for such purpose—and you allow him to make war at pleasure. Study to see if you can fix *any limit* to his power in this respect, after you have given him so much as you propose. If, today, he should choose to

say he thinks it necessary to invade Canada, to prevent the British from invading us, how could you stop him? You may say to him, "I see no probability of the British invading us," but he will say to you, "Be silent; I see it, if you don't."
  —*Letter to William H. Herndon, Lincoln's law partner in Springfield,*
Illinois, February 15, 1848

৯৯

I protest against your calling the condemnation of Polk "opposing the war." In thus assuming that all must be opposed to the war, even though they vote supplies, who do not endorse Polk, with due deference I say I think you fall into one of the artfully set traps of Locofocoism.
  —*Letter to Usher Linder, March 22, 1848*

৯৯

That the Constitution gives the President a negative on legislation, all know; but that this negative should be so combined with plat-forms and other appliances as to enable him and, in fact, almost compel him to take the whole of legislation into his own hands is what we object to—is what General Taylor objects to—and is what constitutes the broad distinction between you and us.
  —*Speech in the U.S. House of Representatives, July 27, 1848*

৯৯

I understand your idea, that if a Presidential candidate avow his opinion upon a given question, or rather upon all questions, and the people, with full knowledge of this, elect him, they thereby distinctly approve all those opinions. This, though plausible, is a most pernicious deception.
  —*Speech in the U.S. House of Representatives, July 27, 1848*

৯৯

A fellow once advertised that he had made a discovery by which he could make a new man out of an old one, and have enough of the stuff left to make a little yellow dog. Just such a discovery has General Jackson's popularity been to you. You not only twice

made President of him out of it, but you have had enough of the stuff left to make Presidents of several comparatively small men since; and it is your chief reliance now to make still another.
—*Speech in the U.S. House of Representatives, July 27, 1848*

ɕ

Mr. Speaker, we have all heard of the animal standing in doubt between two stacks of hay and starving to death; the like of that would never happen to General Cass. Place the stacks a thousand miles apart, he would stand stock-still midway between them and eat them both at once; and the green grass along the line would be apt to suffer some too, at the same time. By all means, make him President, gentlemen. He will feed you bounteously—if—if there is any left after he shall have helped himself.
—*Speech in the U.S. House of Representatives, July 27, 1848.*
(Lincoln had analyzed Cass's accounts from 1813–1831 when he was governor of the Michigan Territory, wherein Cass made daily expense claims from various locales.)

ɕ

The declaration that we have always opposed the war is true or false, accordingly as one may understand the term "opposing the war." If to say "the war was unnecessarily and unconstitutionally commenced by the President," be opposing the war, then the Whigs have very generally opposed it.
—*Speech in the U.S. House of Representatives, July 27, 1848*

ɕ

Stand with anybody that stands *right*. Stand with him while he is right and *part* with him when he goes wrong.
—*Speech, Peoria, Illinois, October 16, 1854*

ɕ

When the white man governs himself that is self-government; but when he governs himself and also governs *another* man, that is *more* than self-government—that is despotism.
—*Speech, Peoria, Illinois, October 16, 1854*

... no man is good enough to govern another man *without that other's consent.*
—*Speech, Peoria, Illinois, October 16, 1854*

Repeal the Missouri Compromise—repeal all compromises—repeal the Declaration of Independence—repeal all past history, you still can not repeal human nature. It still will be the abundance of man's heart that slavery extension is wrong; and out of the abundance of his heart, his mouth will continue to speak.
—*Speech, Peoria, Illinois, October 16, 1854*

The election is over, the session is ended, and I am *not* senator. I have to content myself with the honor of having been the first choice of a large majority of the fifty-one members who finally made the election. My larger number of friends had to surrender to Trumbull's smaller number, in order to prevent the election of Matteson, which would have been a Douglas victory. I started with 44 votes and T. with 5. It was rather hard for the 44 to have to surrender to the 5—and a less good humored man than I perhaps would not have consented to it—and it would not have been done without my consent. I could not, however, let the whole political result go to ruin on a point merely personal to myself.
—*Letter to William H. Henderson, February 21, 1855*

You say if Kansas fairly votes herself a free state, as a Christian you will rather rejoice at it. All decent slaveholders *talk* that way; and I do not doubt their candor. But they never *vote* that way. Although in a private letter or conversation you will express your preference that Kansas shall be free, you would vote for no man for Congress who would say the same thing publicly. No such man could be elected from any district in any slave-state. ... The slave-breeders and slave-traders are a small, odious and detested class among you; and yet in politics, they dictate the course of all of you, and are as completely your masters as you are the master of your own negroes.
—*Letter to Joshua Speed, August 24, 1855*

When the Know-Nothing party first came up, I had an Irishman, Patrick by name, hoeing in my garden. One morning I was there with him, and he said, "Mr. Lincoln, what about the Know-Nothings?" I explained that they would possibly carry a few elections and disappear, and I asked Pat why he was not born in this country. "Faith, Mr. Lincoln," he replied, "I wanted to be, but my mother wouldn't let me."

—*Remark to Richard H. Ballinger, on the nativist, anti-immigrant political party Know-Nothings (n.d.)*

You can fool some of the people all of the time, and all of the people some of the time, but you can't fool all of the people all of the time.

—*Attributed to Lincoln, but never contemporaneously quoted, during his Bloomington, Illinois, speech on May 29, 1856*

Our government rests in public opinion. Whoever can change public opinion can change the government, practically just so much. Public opinion, on any subject, always has a *"central idea,"* from which all its minor thoughts radiate. That "central idea" in our political public opinion at the beginning was and until recently has continued to be, "the equality of men."

—*Speech at a Republican banquet in Chicago, December 10, 1856*

All of us who did not vote for Mr. Buchanan, taken together, are a majority of four hundred thousand. But, in the late contest we were divided between Fremont and Fillmore. Can we not come together, for the future? Let everyone who really believes, and is resolved, that free society is not and *shall not be* a failure, and who can conscientiously declare that in the past contest he has done only what he thought best—let every such one have charity to believe that every other one can say as much. Thus let bygones be bygones. Let past differences, as nothing be; and with steady eye on the real issue, let us reinaugurate the good old "central ideas" of the republic. We *can* do it. The human heart *is* with us—God is with us. We

shall again be able not to declare that "all States as States are equal,"
nor yet that "all citizens as citizens are equal," but to renew the
broader, better declaration, including both these and much more,
that "all *men* are created equal."

—*Speech at a Republican banquet in Chicago, December 10, 1856*

❧

... we think the Dred Scott decision is erroneous. We know the
court that made it has often overruled its own decisions, and we
shall do what we can to have it overrule this.

—*Speech at Springfield, Illinois, June 26, 1857*

❧

The Republicans inculcate, with whatever of ability they can, that
the negro is a man; that his bondage is cruelly wrong, and that the
field of his oppression ought not to be enlarged. The Democrats
deny his manhood; deny, or dwarf to insignificance, the wrong of
his bondage; so far as possible crush all sympathy for him, and
cultivate and excite hatred and disgust against him; compliment
themselves as Union-savers for doing so; and call the indefinite
outspreading of his bondage "a sacred right of self-government."

—*Speech, Springfield, Illinois, June 26, 1857*

❧

I think Greeley is not doing me, an old Republican and a tried
antislavery man, right. He is talking up Douglas, an untrue and
untried man, a dodger, a wriggler, a tool of the South once and
now a snapper at it—hope he will bite 'em good—but I don't feel
that it is exactly right to pull me down in order to elevate Douglas.
I like Greeley, think he intends right, but I think he errs in this
hoisting up of Douglas, while he gives me a downward shove.

—*Remark to William H. Herndon, Lincoln's law partner in
Springfield, Illinois, early 1858*

❧

Whether the Lecompton constitution should be accepted or rejected
is a question upon which, in the minds of men not committed to

any of its antecedents, and controlled only by the Federal Constitution, by republican principles, and by a sound morality, it seems to me there could not be two opinions. It should be throttled and killed as hastily and as heartily as a rabid dog.

—Draft of a speech, c. May 18, 1858

જ

Welcome, or unwelcome, agreeable, or disagreeable, whether this shall be an entire slave nation *is* the issue before us. Every incident—every little shifting of scenes or of actors—only clears away the intervening trash, compacts and consolidates the opposing hosts, and brings them more and more distinctly face to face. The conflict will be a severe one; and it will be fought through by those who *do* care for the result, and not by those who do not care—by those who are for and those who are against a legalized national slavery.

—Draft of a speech, c. May 18, 1858

જ

"A house divided against itself cannot stand."

I believe this government cannot endure, permanently half *slave* and half *free*.

I do not expect the Union to be *dissolved*—I do not expect the house to *fall*—but I *do* expect it will cease to be divided.

It will become *all* one thing or *all* the other.

—Speech accepting the nomination for U.S. Senator, Republican State Convention, Springfield, Illinois, June 16, 1858

જ

The difference between the Republican and the Democratic parties on the leading issues of this contest, as I understand it, is that the former consider slavery a moral, social and political wrong, while the latter *do not* consider it either a moral, social or political wrong; and the action of each, as respects the growth of the country and the expansion of our population, is squared to meet these views.

—Speech, Edwardsville, Illinois, September 11, 1858

The Republican party ... hold that this government was instituted to secure the blessings of freedom, and that slavery is an unqualified evil to the negro, to the white man, to the soil, and to the State.

—*Speech, Edwardsville, Illinois, September 11, 1858*

❧

It is worthwhile to observe that we have generally had comparative peace upon the slavery question and that there has been no cause for alarm until it was excited by the effort to spread it into new territory. Whenever it has been limited to its present bounds and there has been no effort to spread it, there has been peace. All the trouble and convulsion has proceeded from efforts to spread it over more territory.

—*Third debate with Stephen Douglas, Jonesboro, Illinois, September 15, 1858*

❧

Do we have any peace upon the slavery question? Do we have any peace upon it? When are we going to have any peace upon it if it is kept up just now as it is? How are we going to have peace upon it? Why, to be sure, if we will just keep quiet and allow Judge Douglas and his friends to march on and plant slavery in all the States we shall have peace. They have been fussing over it for forty years in the Missouri compromise, in the annexation of Texas, in the acquisition of territory acquired from Mexico, in the war with Mexico, leading to the compromise of 1850, and when it was then settled forever, as both great political parties said it was, that forever turned out to be two years.

—*Debate with Stephen Douglas, rejoinder, Charleston, Illinois, September 18, 1858*

❧

I have insisted that in legislating for a new country where slavery does not exist, there is no just rule other than that of pure morality and pure abstract right; and with reference to legislating with regard to these new countries, this abstract maxim, the right [to] life, lib-

erty and the pursuit of happiness, are the first rules to be considered
and referred to.

—*Debate with Stephen Douglas, reply, Galesburg, Illinois,*
October 7, 1858

◈

... there is a sentiment in the country contrary to me—a sentiment
which holds that slavery is not wrong, and therefore it goes for
policy that does not propose dealing with it as a wrong. That policy
is the Democratic policy, and that sentiment is the Democratic
sentiment. ... Perhaps the Democrat who says he is as much opposed to slavery as I am will tell me that I am wrong about this. I
wish him to examine his own course in regard to this matter a moment, and then see if his opinion will not be changed a little. You
say it is wrong; but don't you constantly object to anybody else
saying so? Do you not constantly argue that this is not the right
place to oppose it? You say it must not be opposed in the free
States, because slavery is not here; it must not be opposed in the
slave States, because it is there; it must not be opposed in politics,
because that will make a fuss; it must not be opposed in the pulpit,
because it is not religion. Then where is the place to oppose it?
There is no suitable place to oppose it. There is no place in the
country to oppose this evil overspreading the continent, which you
say yourself is coming.

—*Sixth debate with Stephen Douglas, Quincy, Illinois,*
October 13, 1858

◈

He reads something from Mr. Buchanan [the president], and undertakes to involve him in an inconsistency, and he gets something
of a cheer on doing so. I would only say to the Judge, now that he
is valiantly fighting for the Nebraska bill and the repeal of the
Missouri compromise, that it is but a little while since he was the
valiant advocate of the Missouri compromise. Now I want to know
if Mr. Buchanan has not as much right to be inconsistent as has
Judge Douglas? Has Judge Douglas an exclusive right to be inconsistent? Has he a monopoly on that subject?

—*Debate with Stephen Douglas, reply, Alton, Illinois,*
October 15, 1858

That quotation ["A house divided against itself cannot stand"], and
the sentiment expressed in it, have been extremely offensive to
Judge Douglas. He has warred upon them as Satan does upon the
Bible.

—Debate with Stephen Douglas, reply, Alton, Illinois,
October 15, 1858

◈

To the best of my judgment I have labored *for* and not *against* the
Union. As I have not felt, so I have not expressed any harsh sentiment towards our Southern brethren. I have constantly declared, as
I really believed, the only difference between them and us is the
difference of circumstances.

—Speech, Springfield, Illinois, October 30, 1858

◈

The [Democrats] of today hold the *liberty* of one man to be absolutely nothing when in conflict with another man's right of *property*.
Republicans, on the contrary, are for both the *man* and the *dollar*,
but in cases of conflict, the man *before* the dollar.

—Letter to H. L. Pierce and others, April 6, 1859

◈

… it is now no child's play to save the principles of Jefferson from
total overthrow in this nation.

One would start with great confidence that he could convince
any sane child that the simpler propositions of Euclid are true; but,
nevertheless, he would fail, utterly, with one who should deny the
definitions of axioms. The principles of Jefferson are the definitions and axioms of free society. And yet they are denied, and
evaded, with no small show of success. One dashingly calls them
"glittering generalities"; another bluntly calls them "self evident
lies"; and still others insidiously argue that they apply only to "superior races."

—Letter to H. L. Pierce and others, April 6, 1859

If the rotten democracy shall be beaten in 1860, it has to be done by the North; no human invention can deprive them of the South. I do not deny that there are as good men in the South as the North; and I guess we will elect one of them if he will allow us to do so on Republican ground.

—Letter to Nathan Sargent, June 23, 1859

ട

I believe there is a genuine popular sovereignty. I think a definition of genuine popular sovereignty, in the abstract, would be about this: That each man shall do precisely as he pleases with himself, and with all those things which exclusively concern him. Applied to government, this principle would be, that a general government shall do all those things which pertain to it, and all the local governments shall do precisely as they please in respect to those matters which exclusively concern them. ... Now what is Judge Douglas' Popular Sovereignty? It is, as a principle, no other than that, if one man chooses to make a slave of another man, neither that other man nor anybody else has a right to object.

—Speech at Columbus, Ohio, September 16, 1859

ട

If I might advise my Republican friends here, I would say to them, leave your Missouri neighbors alone. Have nothing whatever to do with their slaves. Have nothing whatever to do with the white people, save in a friendly way. Drop past differences, and so conduct yourselves that if you cannot be at peace with them, the fault shall be wholly theirs.

—Speech, Leavenworth, Kansas, December 3, 1859

ട

... you [Democrats] are for the Union; and you greatly fear the success of the Republicans would destroy the Union. Why? Do the Republicans declare against the Union? Nothing like it. Your own statement of it is that if the Black Republicans elect a President, you won't stand it. You will break up the Union. That will be your act, not ours. To justify it, you must show that our policy gives you just cause for such desperate action. Can you do that? When you attempt it, you will find that our policy is exactly the policy of the men who made the Union. Nothing more and nothing less.

—*Speech, Leavenworth, Kansas, December 3, 1859*

ც๑

The fact that we get no votes in your section is a fact of your making, and not of ours. And if there be fault in that fact, that fault is primarily yours, and remains until you show that we repel you by some wrong principle or practice.

—*Speech (the "a few words to the Southern people" section) at the Cooper Union Institute, New York City, February 27, 1860*

ც๑

If slavery is right, all words, acts, laws, and constitutions against it are themselves wrong, and should be silenced, and swept away. If it is right, we cannot justly object to its nationality—its universality; if it is wrong, they cannot justly insist upon its extension—its enlargement. All they ask, we could readily grant, if we thought slavery right; all we ask, they could as readily grant, if they thought it wrong. Their thinking it right, and our thinking it wrong, is the precise fact upon which depends the whole controversy. Thinking it right, as they do, they are not to blame for desiring its full recognition, as being right; but, thinking it wrong, as we do, can we yield to them? Can we cast our votes with their view, and against our own? In view of our moral, social, and political responsibilities, can we do this?

—*Speech at the Cooper Union Institute, New York City, February 27, 1860*

ც๑

The new Territories are the newly made bed to which our children are to go, and it lies with the nation to say whether they shall have snakes mixed up with them or not. It does not seem as if there could be much hesitation what our policy should be.

—*Speech, New Haven, Connecticut, March 6, 1860*

Let there be no compromise on the question of *extending* slavery. If there is, all our labor is lost, and, ere long, must be done again. The dangerous ground—that into which some of our friends have a hankering to run—is Popular Sovereignty. Have none of it. Stand firm. The tug has to come, and better now than at any time hereafter.

—*Letter to Senator Lyman Trumbull, December 10, 1860*

❧

Do the people of the South really entertain fears that a Republican administration would, directly or indirectly, interfere with their slaves or with them about their slaves? If they do, I wish to assure you, as once a friend, and still, I hope, not an enemy, that there is no cause for such fears.

—*Letter to Alexander Stephens (future vice president of the Confederate States), December 22, 1860*

❧

Why should there not be patient confidence in the ultimate justice of the people? Is there any better, or equal hope, in the world? In our present differences, is either party without faith of being in the right? If the Almighty Ruler of nations, with his eternal truth and justice, be on your side of the North, or on yours of the South, that truth, and that justice, will surely prevail, by the judgment of this great tribunal, the American people.

—*First inaugural address, March 4, 1861*

❧

... ballots are the rightful and peaceful successors of bullets; and ... when ballots have fairly and constitutionally decided, there can be no successful appeal back to bullets; that there can be no successful appeal, except to ballots themselves, at succeeding elections. Such will be a great lesson of peace: teaching men that what they cannot take by an election, neither can they take it by a war; teaching all the folly of being the beginners of a war.

—*Message to Congress in Special Session, July 4, 1861*

The prudent, penniless beginner in the world labors for wages awhile, saves a surplus with which to buy tools or land for himself, then labors on his own account another while, and at length hires another new beginner to help him. This is the just and generous and prosperous system which opens the way to all—gives hope to all, and consequent energy and progress and improvement of condition to all. No men living are more worthy to be trusted than those who toil up from poverty—none less inclined to take or touch aught which they have not honestly earned. Let them beware of surrendering a political power which they already possess, and which, if surrendered, will surely be used to close the door of advancement against such as they, and to fix new disabilities and burdens upon them, till all of liberty shall be lost.

—*Annual Message to Congress, December 3, 1861*

We have lost the elections; and it is natural that each of us will believe, and say, it has been because his peculiar views was not made sufficiently prominent. I think I know what it was, but I may be mistaken. Three main causes told the whole story. 1. The Democrats were left in a majority by our friends going to the war. 2. The Democrats observed this and determined to reinstate themselves in power, and 3. Our newspapers, by vilifying and disparaging the administration, furnished them all the weapons to do it with. Certainly, the ill success of the war had much to do with this.

—*Letter to General Carl Schurz, November 10, 1862*

In times like the present, men should utter nothing for which they would not willingly be responsible through time and in eternity.

—*Annual Message to Congress, December 1, 1862*

Nothing is likely to be so baleful in the great work before us, as stepping aside of the main object to consider who will get the offices if a small matter shall go thus, and who will get them if it shall go otherwise. It is a time now for real patriots to rise above all this.

—*Letter to Dr. Thomas Cottman of Louisiana, on bringing Louisiana back into the Union, December 15, 1863*

Some of our folks had expressed the opinion that it would be wise to take a War Democrat as candidate for vice president, and that, if possible, a border-state man should be the nominee. ... Andy Johnson, I think, is a good man.

—*Remark to journalist and friend Noah Brooks, after being renominated for president at the Republican National Convention, June 8, 1864*

The opposition politicians are so blinded with rage seeing themselves unable to control the politics of the country that they may be able to manage the Chicago convention for some violent end, but they cannot transfer the people, the honest though misguided masses, to the same course.

—*Remark to his assistant private secretary John Hay, June 17, 1864*

It is much better not to be led from the region of reason into that of hot blood by imputing to public men motives which they do not avow.

—*Remark to his former Postmaster General Montgomery Blair, countering Blair's complaints about the "Radicals" in Congress, December 18, 1864*

POLITICIANS

Henry Clay: "Whatever he did, he did for the whole country"

ତ

Mr. Clay's lack of a more perfect early education, however it may be regretted generally, teaches at least one profitable lesson: it teaches that in this country one can scarcely be so poor but that, if he *will*, he *can* acquire sufficient education to get through the world respectably.

—*Eulogy on Henry Clay, the State House, Springfield, Illinois,
July 6, 1852*

ତ

With other men, to be defeated was to be forgotten; but to him, defeat was but a trifling incident, neither changing him or the world's estimate of him. Even those of both political parties who have been preferred to him for the highest office have run far briefer courses than he, and left him, still shining, high in the heavens of the political world. Jackson, Van Buren, Harrison, Polk, and Taylor all rose *after* and set long before him.

—*Eulogy on Henry Clay, the State House, Springfield, Illinois,
July 6, 1852*

ତ

Mr. Clay's eloquence did not consist, as many fine specimens of eloquence do, of types and figures—of antithesis and elegant arrangement of words and sentences; but rather of that deeply earnest and impassioned tone and manner, which can proceed only from great sincerity and thorough conviction in the speaker of the justice and importance of his cause. This it is, that truly touches the chords of human sympathy; and those who heard Mr. Clay never failed to be moved by it or ever afterwards forgot the impression. All his efforts were made for practical effect. He never spoke merely to be heard.

—*Eulogy on Henry Clay, the State House, Springfield, Illinois,
July 6, 1852*

Whatever he did, he did for the whole country. In the construction of his measures he ever carefully surveyed every part of the field, and duly weighed every conflicting interest. Feeling, as he did, and as the truth surely is, that the world's best hope depended on the continued Union of these States, he was ever jealous of, and watchful for, whatever might have the slightest tendency to separate them.

—Eulogy on Henry Clay, the State House, Springfield, Illinois, July 6, 1852

❧

He loved his country partly because it was his own country, but mostly because it was a free country; and he burned with a zeal for its advancement, prosperity and glory, because he saw in such, the advancement, prosperity and glory of human liberty, human right and human nature. He desired the prosperity of his countrymen partly because they were his countrymen, but chiefly to show to the world that freemen could be prosperous.

—Eulogy on Henry Clay, the State House, Springfield, Illinois, July 6, 1852

❧

Such a man the times have demanded, and such, in the providence of God was given us. But he is gone. Let us strive to deserve, as far as mortals may, the continued care of Divine Providence …

—Eulogy on Henry Clay, the State House, Springfield, Illinois, July 6, 1852

❧

Stephen Douglas: "He never lets the logic of principle displace the logic of success"

❧

It is impossible to get the advantage of him. Even if he is worsted, he so bears himself that the people are bewildered and uncertain as to who has the better of it.

—Remark to William Dickson on the debating skills of Stephen Douglas, September 1855

Douglas is a great man—at keeping from answering questions he don't want to answer.

> —*Speech, Kalamazoo, Michigan, August 27, 1856*

&

With *me*, the race of ambition has been a failure—a flat failure; with *him* it has been one of splendid success. His name fills the nation, and is not unknown even in foreign lands.

> —*Note on Stephen Douglas, c. December 1856*

&

His tactics just now, in part, is to make it appear that he is having a triumphal entry into and march through the country; but it is all as bombastic and hollow as Napoleon's bulletins sent back from his campaign in Russia.

> —*Letter to Gustave Koerner, on Stephen Douglas,*
> *July 15, 1858*

&

Senator Douglas is of worldwide renown. All the anxious politicians of his party, or who have been of his party for years past, have been looking upon him as certainly, at no distant day, to be the President of the United States. They have seen in his round, jolly, fruitful face post offices, land offices, marshal-ships, and cabinet appointments, charge-ships and foreign missions, bursting and sprouting out in wonderful exuberance ready to be laid hold of by their greedy hands. And as they have been gazing upon this attractive picture so long, they cannot, in the little distraction that has taken place in the party, bring themselves to give up the charming hope; but with greedier anxiety they rush about him, sustain him, and give him marches, triumphal entries, and receptions beyond what even in the days of his highest prosperity they could have brought about in his favor. On the contrary, nobody has ever expected me to be President. In my poor, lean, lank face, nobody has ever seen that any cabbages were sprouting out.

> —*Speech, Springfield, Illinois, July 17, 1858*

I am informed that my distinguished friend yesterday became a little excited, nervous, perhaps, and he said something about *fighting*, as though referring to a pugilistic encounter between him and myself. Did anybody in this audience hear him use such language? I am informed, further, that somebody in *his* audience, rather more excited, or nervous, than himself, took off his coat and offered to take the job off Judge Douglas's hands and fight Lincoln himself. Did anybody here witness that warlike proceeding? Well, I merely desire to say that I shall fight neither Judge Douglas nor his second. I shall not do this for two reasons, which I will now explain. In the first place, a fight would *prove* nothing which is in issue in this contest. It might establish that Judge Douglas is a more muscular man than myself, or it might demonstrate that I am a more muscular man than Judge Douglas. But this question is not referred to in the Cincinnati platform, nor in either of the Springfield platforms. Neither result would prove him right or me wrong. And so of the gentleman who volunteered to do his fighting for him. If my fighting Judge Douglas would not prove anything, it would certainly prove nothing for me to fight his bottle-holder.

—*Speech, Havana, Illinois, August 14, 1858*

... I cannot shake Judge Douglas's teeth loose from the Dred Scott decision. Like some obstinate animal (I mean no disrespect) that will hang on when he has once got his teeth fixed, you may cut off a leg, or you may tear away an arm, still he will not relax his hold. And so I may point out to the Judge and say that he is bespattered all over, from the beginning of his political life to the present time, with attacks upon judicial decisions—I may cut off limb after limb of his public record, and strive to wrench him from a single dictum of the Court—yet I cannot divert him from it. He hangs to the last to the Dred Scott decision.

—*First debate with Stephen Douglas, Ottawa, Illinois, August 21, 1858*

Judge Douglas must, when he made that statement, have been crazy—he must have been out of his mind, else he would have

known that the promises, and windy promises, of his power to an-
nihilate Lincoln would not be sustained at all. Now, how much do
I look like being carried away from here? Now, let the Judge come
back on me in his half hour, and I want you, if I can't get away
from here to let me sit here and rot, unless I am able to carry him
to the tavern. What did the Judge think about trotting me here to
Egypt [Illinois] and scaring me to death? Did he suppose that he
would be able to make his friends turn on me and hurt me? I know
this class of people better than he does. I was raised among this
range of people, I am part of this people.
            —*Debate, reply to Stephen Douglas, Jonesboro, Illinois,*
                                    September 15, 1858

                                    ❧

The Judge has set about trying to make the impression that when
we meet, that I am generally in his clutches, that I am a poor de-
crepit mouse, that I cannot do anything at all. I don't know how
to meet that sort of thing. I don't want to call him a liar, yet, if I
come square up to the truth, I do not know what else it is.
            —*Debate, reply to Stephen Douglas, Jonesboro, Illinois,*
                                    September 15, 1858

                                    ❧

Trumbull says it was not in the bill when it went to the committee. When it came back it was in, and Judge Douglas said the al-
terations were made by him in combination with Toombs.
Trumbull alleges therefore as his conclusion that Judge Douglas
put it in. Then if Douglas wants to contradict Trumbull and call
him a liar, let him say he did not put it in, and not that he didn't
take it out again. It is said that a bear is sometimes hard enough
pushed to drop a cub, and so I presume it was in this case. I presume the truth is that Douglas put it in and afterwards took it out.
            —*Fourth debate with Stephen Douglas, on the Toombs Bill,*
                        Charleston, Illinois, September 18, 1858

                                    ❧

You all heard me call upon him to say *which of these pieces of evidence
was a forgery*? Does he say what I present as a copy of the bill re-

ported by himself is a forgery? ... *I would then like to know how it comes about, that when each piece of a story is true, the whole story turns out false.* I take it these people have some sense; they see plainly that Judge Douglas is playing cuttlefish, a small species of fish that has no mode of defending itself when pursued except by throwing out a black fluid, which makes the water so dark the enemy cannot see it and thus it escapes. Ain't the Judge playing the cuttlefish?

—*Fourth debate with Stephen Douglas, on the Toombs Bill, Charleston, Illinois, September 18, 1858*

❧

In his numerous speeches now being made in Illinois, Senator Douglas regularly argues against the doctrine of the equality of men; and while he does not draw the conclusion that the superiors ought to enslave the inferiors, he evidently wishes his hearers to draw that conclusion. He shirks the responsibility of pulling the house down, but he digs under it that it may fall of its own weight.

—*Note, c. October 1, 1858*

❧

A very large portion of the speech which Judge Douglas has addressed to you has previously been delivered and put in print. I did not mean that for a hit upon the Judge at all. If not interrupted, I was going to say that such an answer as I was going to make to a very large portion of it had already been once made and put in print ...

—*Debate with Stephen Douglas, reply, Galesburg, Illinois, October 7, 1858*

❧

The Judge assumes—when he says that I make speeches of one sort for the North and of another sort for the South—he assumes that I do not understand that my speeches will be put in print. Now I have understood that the speeches I made in Chicago, at Jonesboro and at Charleston, would be put in print, and that all reading men might read them, and I have not at all supposed—I do not today suppose—that there is any conflict in them.

—*Debate with Stephen Douglas, reply, Galesburg, Illinois, October 7, 1858*

I see the day rapidly approaching, whatever the result of this
ephemeral contest may be between Judge Douglas and myself—I
see the day fast approaching when his epithets that he has been
cramming down Republican throats will be crammed down his
throat.
                    —*Debate with Stephen Douglas, reply, Galesburg, Illinois,*
                                                        October 7, 1858

ॐ

[Thomas L.] Harris and Douglas were both in Springfield when
that convention was in session, and, although they both left before
the fraud appeared in the Register, subsequent events show that
they both had their eyes constantly fixed upon that convention.
The fraud having been apparently successful upon that occasion,
both Harris and Douglas have more than once been attempting to
put it to new uses, as the woman said when her husband's body was
brought home full of eels, and she was asked what should be done
with him, she said take the eels out and set him again; and so Harris
and Douglas have shown a disposition to take the eels out of that
stale fraud by which they got the first election, and set that fraud
again ...
                    —*Debate with Stephen Douglas, reply, Galesburg, Illinois,*
                                                        October 7, 1858

ॐ

Judge Douglas declares that if any community want slavery they
have a right to have it. He can say that logically, if he says that there
is no wrong in slavery; but if you admit that there is a wrong in it,
he cannot logically say that anybody has a right to do wrong.
                    —*Fifth debate with Stephen Douglas, Galesburg, Illinois,*
                                                        October 7, 1858

ॐ

And I do think ... that Judge Douglas, and whoever like him
teaches that the negro has no share, humble though it may be, in
the Declaration of Independence, is going back to the era of our
liberty and independence, and, so far as in him lies, muzzling the

cannon that thunders its annual joyous return; that he is blowing out the moral lights around us when he contends that whoever wants slaves has a right to hold them; that he is penetrating, so far as lies in his power, the human soul, and eradicating the light of reason and the love of liberty when he is in every possible way preparing the public mind, by his vast influence, for making the institution of slavery perpetual and national.

—*Fifth debate with Stephen Douglas, Galesburg, Illinois,*
October 7, 1858

❧

Judge Douglas asks you, "Why cannot the institution of slavery, or rather, why cannot the nation, part slave and part free, continue as our fathers made it *forever*?" In the first place, I insist that our fathers *did not* make this nation half slave and half free, or part slave and part free. I insist that they found the institution of slavery existing here. They did not make it so, but they left it so because they knew of no way to get rid of it at that time. When Judge Douglas undertakes to say that as a matter of choice the fathers of the government made this nation part slave and part free, *he assumes what is historically a falsehood.*

—*Sixth debate with Stephen Douglas, Quincy, Illinois,*
October 13, 1858

❧

The fight must go on. The cause of civil liberty must not be surrendered at the end of one or even one hundred defeats. Douglas had the ingenuity to be supported in the late contest both as the best means to break down, and to uphold the slave interest. No ingenuity can keep those antagonistic elements in harmony long. Another explosion will soon come.

—*Letter to Henry Asbury, after the election of Douglas,*
November 19, 1858

❧

Another "blow-up" is coming; and we shall have fun again. Douglas managed to be supported both as the best instrument to

put down and to uphold the slave power; but no ingenuity can long
keep these antagonisms in harmony.

—*Letter to Charles Ray, November 20, 1858*

જ

He never lets the logic of principle displace the logic of success.

—*Note for a speech on Stephen Douglas, c. September 1859*

જ

Douglas's position leads to the nationalization of slavery as surely as
does that of Jeff Davis [of Mississippi, future president of the
Confederacy] and [James] Mason of Virginia. The two positions are
but slightly different roads to the same place—with this difference,
that the nationalization of slavery can be reached by Douglas's
route, and never can by the other.

—*Notes for his speeches at Columbus and Cincinnati, Ohio,*
September 16–17, 1859

જ

I understand that he [Douglas] has never said, as an individual,
whether he thought slavery right or wrong—and he is the only
man in the nation that has not! Now such a policy may have a
temporary run; it may spring up as necessary to the political pros-
pects of some gentleman; but it is utterly baseless; the people are
not indifferent; and it can therefore have no durability or perma-
nence.

—*Speech, New Haven, Connecticut, March 6, 1860*

જ

Zachary Taylor: "he seems ... to have conquered by the exercise of a sober and steady judgment"

જ

General Taylor's battles were not distinguished for brilliant military
maneuvers; but in all, he seems rather to have conquered by the

exercise of a sober and steady judgment, coupled with a dogged incapacity to understand that defeat was possible. His rarest military trait was a combination of negatives—absence of *excitement* and absence of *fear*. He could not be *flurried*, and he could not be *scared*.

—*Eulogy on Zachary Taylor, Chicago, July 24, 1850*

The Presidency, even to the most experienced politicians, is no bed of roses; and General Taylor, like others, found thorns within it. No human being can fill that station and escape censure. Still I hope and believe when General Taylor's official conduct shall come to be viewed in the calm light of history, he will be found to have *deserved* as little as any who have succeeded him.

—*Eulogy on Zachary Taylor, Chicago, July 24, 1850*

... the American people, in electing General Taylor to the Presidency, thereby showing their high appreciation of his sterling but unobtrusive qualities, did their *country* a service, and *themselves* an imperishable honor. It is for the young to know that treading the hard path of duty, as he trod it, *will* be noticed, and *will* lead to high places.

—*Eulogy on Zachary Taylor, Chicago, July 24, 1850*

THE PRESIDENCY

... what's the use of talking of me for the presidency, whilst we have such men as Seward, Chase, and others, who are so much better known to the people and whose names are so intimately associated with the principles of the Republican party. Everybody knows them; nobody, scarcely, outside of Illinois, knows me. Besides, is it not, as a matter of justice, due to such men, who have carried this movement forward to its present status, in spite of fearful opposition, personal abuse, and hard names? I really think so.

—*Remark to Illinois politician Jesse W. Fell, 1858*

❧

… I must in candor say I do not think myself fit for the presidency. I certainly am flattered and gratified that some partial friends think of me in that connection; but I really think it best for our cause that no concerted effort, such as you suggest, should be made.

—*Letter to T. J. Pickett, April 16, 1859*

❧

For my single self, I have enlisted for the permanent success of the Republican cause; and, for this object, I shall labor faithfully in the ranks, unless, as I think not probable, the judgment of the party shall assign me a different position.

—*Letter to William Frazer, November 1, 1859*

❧

Now, look here, Mr. Bowen, I am not going to make a failure at the Cooper Institute to-morrow night, if I can possibly help it. I am anxious to make a success of it on account of the young men who have so kindly invited me here. It is on my mind all the time, and I cannot be persuaded to accept your hospitality at this time. Please excuse me and let me go to my room at the hotel, lock the door, and there think about my lecture.

—*Remark to Henry Bowen, on the Cooper Union Institute speech that led to his Republican party nomination for president, February 26, 1860*

❧

The speech at New York, being within my calculation before I started, went off passably well, and gave me no trouble whatever. The difficulty was to make nine others, before reading audiences, who have already seen all my ideas in print.

—*Letter to his wife Mary, from Exeter, New Hampshire,*
March 4, 1860

My name is new in the field; and I suppose I am not the *first* choice of a very great many. Our policy, then, is to give no offence to others—leave them in a mood to come to us, if they shall be compelled to give up their first love.

—*Letter to Samuel Galloway, March 24, 1860*

❧

As you request, I will be entirely frank. The taste *is* in my mouth a little; and this, no doubt, disqualifies me, to some extent, to form correct opinions. You may confidently rely, however, that by no advice or consent of mind shall my pretensions be pressed to the point of endangering our common cause.

—*Letter to Senator Lyman Trumbull, April 29, 1860*

❧

Gentlemen, you had better come up and shake my hand while you can—honors elevate some men.

—*Remark to his friends, on receiving news of the Republican nomination for President, May 18, 1860*

❧

Imploring the assistance of Divine Providence, and with due regard to the views and feelings of all who were represented in the Convention; to the rights of all the states, and territories, and people of the nation; to the inviolability of the Constitution, and the perpetual union, harmony, and prosperity of all, I am most happy to cooperate for the practical success of the principles declared by the Convention.

—*Letter accepting the presidential nomination, to George Ashmun, President of the Republican National Convention, May 23, 1860*

❧

... for personal considerations I would rather have a full term in the Senate—a place in which I would feel more consciously able to discharge the duties required, and where there is more chance to make a reputation, and less danger of losing it—than four years of the presidency.

—*Remark to a New York visitor, October 25, 1860*

❧

I know the justness of my intentions and the utter groundlessness of the pretended fears of the men who are filling the country with their clamor. If I go into the presidency, they will find me as I am on record—nothing less, nothing more.

—*Remark to a newspaper reporter on the Southern reaction to his election, November 14, 1860*

❧

I thank you, in common with all others, who have thought fit, by their votes, to endorse the Republican cause. I rejoice with you in the success which has, so far, attended that cause. Yet in all our rejoicing let us neither express, nor cherish, any harsh feeling towards any citizen who, by his vote, has differed with us. Let us at all times remember that all American citizens are brothers of a common country, and should dwell together in the bonds of fraternal feeling.

—*Remarks to "friends and fellow-citizens," Springfield, Illinois, November 20, 1860*

❧

I don't want to go before the middle of February, because I expect they will drive me insane after I get there, and I want to keep tolerably sane, at least until after the inauguration.

—*Remark to a newspaper reporter on his impending travel to Washington, December 14, 1860*

❧

May I be pardoned if I ask whether even you have ever attempted to procure the reading of the Republican platform, or my speeches, by the Southern people? If not, what reason have I to expect that any additional production of mine would meet a better fate? It would make me appear as if I repented for the crime of having been elected, and was anxious to apologize and beg forgiveness.

—*Letter to Congressman John A. Gilmer of North Carolina,*
December 15, 1860

 و

By no act or complicity of mine shall the Republican party become a mere sucked egg, all shell and no principle in it.

—*Remark to Charles Sumner, January 1861*

 و

I will suffer death before I will consent or will advise my friend to consent to any concession or compromise which looks like buying the privilege to take possession of this government to which we have a constitutional right.

—*Remark to a journalist from the* New York Herald,
January 28, 1861

 و

I think when the clouds look as dark as they do now, one term might satisfy any man.

—*Remark to a newspaper reporter on being asked for his plans to run for*
a second term in four years, February 1861

 و

It seems to me that Douglas got the best of it at the election last fall. I am left to face an empty treasury and a great rebellion, while my own party endorses his popular sovereignty idea and applies it in legislation. ... I only wish I could have got there to lock the door before the horse was stolen. But when I get to the spot, I can find the tracks.

—*Remarks to his friend Joseph Gillespie, as he left for*
Washington, D.C., February 11, 1861

I, as already intimated, am but an accidental instrument, temporary, and to serve but for a limited time, but I appeal to you again to constantly bear in mind that with you, and not with politicians, not with Presidents, not with office-seekers, but with you, is the question, "Shall the Union and shall the liberties of this country be preserved to the latest generation?"

—*Speech, from the platform of his train, to Governor Oliver Morton and the citizens of Indiana, February 11, 1861*

❧

I have been selected to fill an important office for a brief period, and am now, in your eyes, invested with an influence which will soon pass away; but should my administration prove to be a very wicked one, or what is more probable, a very foolish one, if you, the people, are but true to yourselves and to the Constitution, there is but little harm I can do, *thank God!*

—*Speech to his "fellow-countrymen," Lawrenceburg, Indiana, February 12, 1861*

❧

It is true that while I hold myself without mock modesty the humblest of all individuals that have ever been elevated to the Presidency, I have a môre difficult task to perform than any one of them.

—*Speech to the New York State Legislature, Albany, New York, February 18, 1861*

❧

I shall endeavor to take the ground I deem most just to the North, the East, the West, the South, and the whole country. I take it, I hope, in good temper—certainly with no malice toward any section. I shall do all that may be in my power to promote a peaceful settlement of all our difficulties. The man does not live who is more devoted to peace than I am. None who would do more to preserve it. But it may be necessary to put the foot down firmly. And if I do my duty, and do right, you will sustain me, will you not?

—*Speech to the New Jersey State Assembly, February 21, 1861*

It shall be my endeavor to preserve the peace of this country so far as it can possibly be done, consistently with the maintenance of the institutions of the country. With my consent, or without my great displeasure, this country shall never witness the shedding of one drop of blood in fraternal strife.

—*Speech to Governor Andrew Curtin and the citizens of Harrisburg, Pennsylvania, February 22, 1861*

৯৯

... I would rather be assassinated on this spot than to surrender it.

—*Speech at Independence Hall, Philadelphia, February 22, 1861*

৯৯

While the people retain their virtue and vigilance, no administration, by any extreme of wickedness or folly, can very seriously injure the government in the short space of four years.

—*First inaugural address, March 4, 1861*

৯৯

This handshaking is harder work than rail-splitting.

—*Remark to a New York journalist at the inauguration ball, March 4, 1861*

৯৯

I don't know anything about diplomacy. I will be very apt to make blunders.

—*Remark to Rudolf Schleiden, Minister from Bremen, March 1861*

৯৯

I have called this Congress because I must have money. There is Chase; sometimes he calls for a million of dollars in the course of twenty-four hours, and I can assure you that it is not an easy matter to raise that amount in a day. The result of this way is a question of resources. That side will win in the end where the money holds out longest; but if the war should continue until it has cost us five hundred millions of dollars, the resources of the country are such that the credit of the government will be better than it was at the close of the War of the Revolution, with the comparatively small debt that existed then.

—*Remark to Thomas M. Clark, member of the Sanitary Commission,*
Spring 1861

❧

If I were to try to read, much less answer, all the attacks made on me, this shop might as well be closed for any other business. I do the very best I know how—the very best I can; and I mean to keep doing so until the end. If the end brings me out all right, what is said against me won't amount to anything. If the end brings me out wrong, ten thousand angels swearing I was right would make no difference.

—*Remark to an officer suggesting the President refute "an attack made*
on him by the Congressional Committee on the Conduct
of the War" (n.d.)

❧

I pass my life in preventing the storm from blowing down the tent, and I drive in the pegs as fast as they are pulled up.

—*Remark to the French visitor Prince de Joinville,*
c. September 20, 1861

❧

Can it be pretended that it is any longer the government of the U.S.—any government of constitution and laws,—wherein a General or a President, may make permanent rules of property by proclamation?

—*Letter to Orville Browning, September 22, 1861*

❧

Men moving only in an official circle are apt to become merely official, not to say arbitrary, in their ideas, and are apter and apter, with each passing day, to forget that they only hold power in a

representative capacity. Now this is all wrong. I go into these pro-
miscuous receptions of all who claim to have business with me
twice each week, and every applicant for audience has to take his
turn as if waiting to be shaved in a barber's shop. Many of the matters brought to my notice are utterly frivolous, but others are of
more or less importance, and all serve to renew in me a clearer and
more vivid image of that great popular assemblage, out of which I
spring, and to which at the end of two years I must return. I tell
you, Major, that I call these receptions my public-opinion baths;
for I have but little time to read the papers and gather public opinion that way, and though they may not be pleasant in all their
particulars, the effect as a whole is renovating and invigorating to
my perceptions of responsibility and duty.

—*Remark to the officer and writer Charles G. Halpine, c. 1862*

❧

Chase, never regret what you don't write; it is what you do write
that you are often called upon to feel sorry for.

—*Remark to Treasury Secretary Salmon P. Chase, May 1862*

❧

I am a patient man, always willing to forgive on the Christian terms
of repentance, and also to give ample time for repentance; still I
must save this Government if possible. What I *cannot* do, of course,
I will *not* do; but it may as well be understood, once for all, that I
shall not surrender this game leaving any available card unplayed.

—*Letter to Reverdy Johnson, July 26, 1862*

❧

If there be those who would not save the Union unless they could
at the same time destroy slavery, I do not agree with them. My
paramount object in this struggle is to save the Union, and is not
either to save or destroy slavery. If I could save the Union without
freeing any slave, I would do it; and if I could save it by freeing all
the slaves, I would do it; and if I could save it by freeing some and
leaving others alone, I would also do that. What I do about slavery
and the colored race, I do because I believe it helps to save the

Union; and what I forbear, I forbear because I do not believe it would help to save the Union.

> —*Letter to Horace Greeley in response to Greeley's* New York Tribune *editorial "The Prayer of Twenty Millions,"*
> *August 22, 1862*

❧

Well, I would be very happy to oblige you, if my passes were respected; but the fact is, sir, that I have within the last two years given passes to two hundred and fifty thousand men to go to Richmond, and not one has got there yet.

> —*Remark to "a gentleman" who had "solicited a pass for*
> *Richmond" (n.d.)*

❧

If he becomes president, all right, I hope we may never have a worse man. I have all along clearly seen his plan of strengthening himself. Whenever he sees that an important matter is troubling me, if I am compelled to decide it in a way to give offense to a man of some influence, he always ranges himself in opposition to me and persuades the victim that he has been hardly dealt by and that he [Chase] would have arranged it very differently. It was so with General Fremont, with General Hunter when I annulled his hasty proclamation, with General Butler when he was recalled from New Orleans with these Missouri people when they called the other day. I am entirely indifferent as to his success or failure in these schemes, so long as he does his duty as the head of the Treasury Department.

> —*Remark on Secretary of the Treasury Salmon P. Chase to his assistant*
> *private secretary William O. Stoddard, October 18, 1862*

❧

Fellow-citizens, we cannot escape history. We of this Congress and this administration will be remembered in spite of ourselves. No personal significance, or insignificance, can spare one or another of us. The fiery trial through which we pass will light us down, in honor or dishonor, to the latest generation. We *say* we are for the Union. The world will not forget that we say this. We know how to save the Union. The world knows we do know how to save it. We—even *we here*—hold the power and bear the responsibility. In giving freedom to the slave, we *assure* freedom to the *free*—honorable alike in what we give and what we preserve. We shall nobly save or meanly lose the last, best hope of earth. Other means may succeed; this could not fail. The way is plain, peaceful, generous, just—a way which, if followed, the world will forever applaud, and God must forever bless.

—*Annual Message to Congress, December 1, 1862*

❧

As a pilot, I have used my best exertions to keep afloat our ship of State, and shall be glad to resign my trust at the appointed time to another pilot more skillful and successful than I may prove. In every case, and at all hazards, the Government must be perpetuated. Relying, as I do, upon the Almighty Power, and encouraged as I am by these resolutions which you have just read, with the support which I receive from Christian men, I shall not hesitate to use all the means at my control to secure the termination of this rebellion, and will hope for success.

—*Reply to a committee from the Presbyterian General Assembly,*
June 2, 1863

❧

I have here some papers which I started in this morning to carefully examine. They contain the entire proceedings of a military court for the trial of a young soldier for desertion. And they contain minutes of the testimony taken on the trial, together with the conviction and sentence to death of the boy. I have read just three pages of the testimony, and have found this: "The boy said when first arrested that he was going home to see his mother." I don't think that I can allow a boy to be shot who tried to go home to see his mother. I guess I don't want to read any more of this.

—*Remark to Minnesota Senator Morton Smith Wilkinson,*
Summer 1863

My dear man, if your son lives until I order him shot, he will live longer than ever Methuselah did.
—*Remark to a man whose son's execution Lincoln had suspended (n.d.)*

৯৯

I cannot be shut up in an iron cage and guarded. If I have business at the War Office, I must take my hat and go there, and if to kill me is within the purposes of this rebellion, no precaution can prevent it. You may guard me at a single point, but I will necessarily be exposed at others. People come to see me every day and I receive them, and I do not know but that some of them are secessionists or engaged in plots to kill me. The truth is, if any man has made up his mind that he will give his life for mine, he can take mine.
—*Remark to Leonard Swett, Summer 1863*

৯৯

Well, I've got something now that I can give to everybody.
—*Remark after catching varioloid, a contagious disease, c. December 1863*

৯৯

How willingly would I exchange places today with the soldier who sleeps on the ground in the Army of the Potomac.
—*Remark to Schuyler Colfax, Speaker of the House, 1863*

৯৯

Mr. Seward is limited to a couple of stories which from repeating he believes are true.
—*Remark to a soldier, 1863*

৯৯

I desire to so conduct the affairs of this administration that if, at the end, when I come to lay down the reins of power, I have lost every other friend on earth, I shall at least have one friend left, and that friend shall be down inside of me.
—*Remark to a delegation of Missouri and Kansas "Radicals,"*
September 30, 1863

Let him alone; he can do no more harm in here than he can outside.
—*Remark to an Illinois lawyer, who suggested Lincoln remove Salmon P. Chase from his position as Treasury Secretary, February 1864*

∽

A traveler on the frontier found himself out of his reckoning one night in a most inhospitable region. A terrific thunderstorm came up to add to his trouble. He floundered along until his horse at length gave out. The lightning afforded him the only clue to his way, but the peals of thunder were frightful. One bolt, which seemed to crash the earth beneath him, brought him to his knees. By no means a praying man, his petition was short and to the point—"O Lord, if it is all the same to you, give us a little more light and a little less noise!"
—*Remark to his portrait painter, Francis B. Carpenter, on newspaper criticism, March 2, 1864*

∽

Soon after I was nominated at Chicago, I began to receive letters threatening my life. The first one or two made me a little uncomfortable, but I came at length to look for a regular installment of this kind of correspondence in every week's mail, and up to inauguration day I was in constant receipt of such letters. It is no uncommon thing to receive them now; but they have ceased to give me any apprehension. ... there is nothing like getting used to things!
—*Remark on news of a Confederate plot to kidnap or murder him, to his portrait painter, Francis B. Carpenter, late March, 1864*

∽

A year or two after Tyler's accession to the presidency, contemplating an excursion in some direction, his son went to order a special train of cars. It so happened that the railroad superintendent was a very strong Whig. On Bob's making known his errand, that official bluntly informed him that his road did not run any special trains for the president. "What," said Bob, "did you not furnish a special train for the funeral of General Harrison?" "Yes," said the

superintendent, stroking his whiskers, "and if you will only bring
your father here in *that* shape, you shall have the best train on the
road."

—*Remark to his portrait painter, Francis B. Carpenter, spring 1864*

❧

I have not permitted myself, gentlemen, to conclude that I am the
best man in the country; but I am reminded, in this connection, of
a story of an old Dutch farmer, who remarked to a companion once
that "it was not best to swap horses when crossing streams."

—*Reply to a delegation from the National Union League,*
June 9, 1864

❧

This is the third time he has thrown this at me, and I do not think
I am called on to continue to beg him to take it back, especially
when the country would not go to destruction in consequence. ...
On the whole, Brough, I reckon you had better let it alone this
time.

—*Remark to Ohio governor John Brough, on Secretary of the Treasury*
Salmon P. Chase's offered resignation, June 1864

❧

Your resignation of the office of Secretary of the Treasury, sent me
yesterday, is accepted. Of all I have said in commendation of your
ability and fidelity, I have nothing to unsay; and yet you and I have
reached a point of mutual embarrassment in our official relation
which it seems can not be overcome, or longer sustained, consistently with the public service.

—*Letter to Salmon P. Chase, June 30, 1864*

❧

Of Mr. Chase's ability and of his soundness on the general issues of
the war there is, of course, no question. I have only one doubt
about his appointment. He is a man of unbounded ambition and
has been working all his life to become president. That he can

never be, and I fear that if I make him chief justice, he will simply become more restless and uneasy and neglect the place in his strife and intrigue to make himself president. If I were sure that he would go on the bench and give up his aspirations and do nothing but make himself a great judge, I would not hesitate a moment.

—Remark to Senator Henry Wilson of Massachusetts, who was advocating Salmon P. Chase's appointment as Chief Justice of the Supreme Court, August 1864

❧

I happen temporarily to occupy this big White House. I am a living witness that any one of your children may look to come here as my father's child has. It is in order that each of you may have through this free government which we have enjoyed an open field and a fair chance for your industry, enterprise and intelligence; that you may all have equal privileges in the race of life, with all its desirable human aspirations. It is for this the struggle should be maintained, that we may not lose our birthright—not only for one, but for two or three years. The nation is worth fighting for to secure such an inestimable jewel.

—Speech to 166th Ohio Regiment, August 22, 1864

❧

This morning, as for some days past, it seems exceedingly probable that this Administration will not be reelected. Then it will be my duty to so cooperate with the President-elect as to save the Union between the election and the inauguration; as he will have secured his election on such ground that he cannot possibly save it afterwards.

—Memorandum, August 23, 1864

❧

You think I don't know I am going to be beaten, *but I do*, and unless some great change takes place, *badly beaten*.

—Remark on the coming presidential election, August 1864. (This "great change" took place, most notably through General William T. Sherman's taking of Atlanta in early September.)

I confess that I desire to be re-elected. God knows I do not want the labor and responsibility of the office for another four years. But I have the common pride of humanity to wish my past four years Administration endorsed.

—Remark, c. 1864

୨ଡ଼

It is my conviction that, had the Proclamation been issued even six months earlier than it was, public sentiment would not have sustained it. Just so as to the subsequent action in reference to enlisting blacks in the border states. The step, taken sooner, could not, in my judgment, have been carried out. A man watches his pear tree day after day, impatient for the ripening of the fruit. Let him attempt to force the process, and he may spoil both fruit and tree. But let him patiently wait, and the ripe pear at length falls into his lap. We have seen this great revolution in public sentiment slowly but surely progressing, so that, when final action came, the opposition was not strong enough to defeat the purpose.

—Remark to his portrait painter Francis Carpenter, 1864

୨ଡ଼

Oh, dear, dear! These cases kill me! I wish I didn't have to hear about them! What shall I do? You make the laws, and then you come with heartbroken women and ask me to set them aside. You have decided that if a soldier raises his hand against his superior officer, as this man has done, he shall die! Then if I leave the laws to be executed, one of these distressing scenes occurs, which almost kills me.

—Remark to Congressmen who had just witnessed a woman's appeal for
a commutation of her husband's death sentence (n.d.)

୨ଡ଼

Some of my generals complain that I impair discipline and subordination in the army by my pardons and respites, but it makes me rested after a day's hard work if I can find some good excuse for saving a man's life, and I go to bed happy as I think how joyous the signing of my name will make him and his family and friends.

—Remark to Schuyler Colfax, Speaker of the House of
Representatives, c. 1864

To remove a man is very easy, but when I go to fill his place, there are twenty applicants, and of these I must make nineteen enemies.
> —*Remark to his portrait painter Francis Carpenter, c. 1864*

⚮

The fact is … I have got more pigs than I have teats.
> —*Remark on political patronage to*
> *Congressman Luther Hanchett (n.d.)*

⚮

The chickens of the family got so used to being moved that whenever they saw the wagon sheets brought out, they laid themselves on their backs and crossed their legs, ready to be tied. Now, gentlemen, if I were to listen to every committee that comes in that door, I had just as well cross my hands and let you tie me. Nevertheless, I am glad to see you.
> —*Remark to a delegation from Ohio (n.d.)*

⚮

I am struggling to maintain government, not to overthrow it. I am struggling especially to prevent others from overthrowing it. I therefore say, that if I shall live, I shall remain President until the fourth of next March; and that whoever shall be constitutionally elected therefore in November shall be duly installed as President on the fourth of March; and that in the interval I shall do my utmost that whoever is to hold the helm for the next voyage shall start with the best possible chance to save the ship.
> —*Response to a serenade by a group of Maryland citizens,*
> *October 19, 1864*

⚮

It does look as if the people wanted me to stay here a little longer, and I suppose I shall have to, if they do.
> —*Remark overheard by the diarist George Templeton*
> *Strong, 1864*

Being only mortal, after all, I should have been a little mortified if I had been beaten in this canvas before the people; but that sting would have been more than compensated by the thought that the people had notified me that all my official responsibilities were soon to be lifted off my back.

—*Remark to journalist and friend Noah Brooks,*
November 9, 1864

༅

We can not have free government without elections; and if the rebellion could force us to forego, or postpone, a national election, it might fairly claim to have already conquered and ruined us. The strife of the election is but human-nature practically applied to the facts of the case. What has occurred in this case must ever recur in similar cases. Human-nature will not change. In any future great national trial compared with the men of this, we shall have as weak, and as strong; as silly and as wise; as bad and good. Let us, therefore, study the incidents of this, as philosophy to learn wisdom from, and none of them as wrongs to be revenged.

—*Address to a congratulatory serenade on his reelection,*
November 10, 1864

༅

... now that the election is over, may not all, having a common interest, reunite in a common effort, to save our common country? For my own part I have striven, and shall strive to avoid placing any obstacle in the way. So long as I have been here I have not willingly planted a thorn in any man's bosom. While I am deeply sensible to the high compliment of a re-election; and duly grateful, as I trust, to Almighty God for having directed my countrymen to a right conclusion, as I think, for their own good, it adds nothing to my satisfaction that any other man may be disappointed or pained by the result.

—*Address to a congratulatory serenade on his reelection,*
November 10, 1864

I should be the veriest shallow and self-conceited blockhead upon the footstool if, in my discharge of the duties which are put upon me in this place, I should hope to get along without the wisdom which comes from God and not from men.
—*Remark to journalist and friend Noah Brooks, three days after his second presidential election, November 11, 1864*

ও

My cabinet has shrunk up North, and I must find a southern man. I suppose if the twelve apostles were to be chosen nowadays, the shrieks of locality would have to be heeded.
—*Remark to Assistant Attorney General Titian J. Coffey, November 1864*

ও

Although I may be stronger as an authority, yet if all the rest oppose, I must give way. Old Hickory, who had as much iron in his neck as anybody, did so sometimes. If the strongest horse in the team would go ahead, he cannot, if all the rest hold back.
—*Remark to Francis Preston Blair, Sr., on appointing a Supreme Court justice, November 1864*

ও

Chase is, on the whole, a pretty good fellow and a very able man. His only trouble is that he has "the White House fever" a little too bad, but I hope this may cure him and that he will be satisfied.
—*Remark to John B. Alley, Republican Congressman, after Lincoln nominated Salmon P. Chase as chief justice of the Supreme Court, December 6, 1864*

ও

Having served four years in the depths of a great, and yet unended national peril, I can view this call to a second term, in nowise more flatteringly to myself, than as an expression of the public judgment that I may better finish a difficult work in which I have labored from the first, than could anyone less severely schooled to the task.

> —*Reply to Representative James Wilson of Iowa, Senator Lyman Trumbull and Representative John Dawson of Pennsylvania, who comprised a committee that officially informed him of his second election as President, March 1, 1865*

ও

How happy, four years hence, will I be to return there in peace and tranquility!

> —*Remark to Charles Adolphe Pineton on the contemplation of returning home to Springfield, Illinois, early April 1865*

ও

READING AND WRITING

When I read aloud two senses catch the idea: first, I see what I read; second, I hear it, and therefore I can remember it better.

> —*Remark to William H. Herndon, his friend and law partner, who asked him, with annoyance, why he read aloud (n.d.)*

ও

I cannot read generally. I never read textbooks, for I have no particular motive to drive and whip me to it. I don't and can't remember such reading.

> —*Remark to William Herndon (n.d.)*

ও

It's like the lazy preacher that used to write long sermons, and the explanation was, he got to writin', and was too lazy to stop.

> —*Remark in court, after a judge wondered at the length of a lawyer's brief, Bloomington, Illinois, 1854–1855*

Well, for those who like that sort of thing, I should think it is just the sort of thing they would like.

> —*Remark to an author who had read him a manuscript on*
> *"an abstruse subject" (n.d.)*

❧

Writing—the art of communicating thoughts to the mind, through the eye—is the great invention of the world.

> —*Lecture, "Discoveries and Inventions," Jacksonville, Illinois,*
> *February 11, 1859*

❧

A capacity and taste for reading gives access to whatever has already been discovered by others. It is the key, or one of the keys, to the already solved problems. And not only so, it gives a relish and facility for successfully pursuing the yet unsolved ones.

> —*Speech to the Wisconsin State Agricultural Society, Milwaukee,*
> *Wisconsin, September 30, 1859*

❧

It is very common in this country to find great facility of expression and less common to find great lucidity of thought. The combination of the two in one person is very uncommon; but whenever you do find it, you have a great man.

> —*Remark to British journalist Edward Dicey, c. 1862–1863*

❧

I can always tell more about a thing after I've heard it read aloud and know how it sounds. Just the reading of it to myself doesn't answer as well either. ... What I want is an audience. Nothing sounds the same when there isn't anybody to hear it and find fault with it.

> —*Remark to William O. Stoddard, a White House*
> *secretary (n.d.)*

I think nothing equals *Macbeth*. It is wonderful. Unlike you gentlemen of the profession, I think the soliloquy in *Hamlet* commencing "O, my offence is rank" surpasses that commencing "To be, or not to be." But pardon this small attempt at criticism.

> —*Letter to the actor James H. Hackett, August 17, 1863*

ও

It matters not to me whether Shakespeare be well or ill acted, with him the thought suffices.

> —*Remark to his portrait painter, Francis B. Carpenter,*
> *early 1864*

ও

It may seem somewhat strange to say, but I never read an entire novel in my life. ... I once commenced *Ivanhoe*, but never finished it.

> —*Remark to his portrait painter, Francis B. Carpenter,*
> *late March 1864*

ও

With educated people, I suppose, punctuation is a matter of rule; with me it is a matter of feeling. But I must say that I have a great respect for the semicolon; it's a very useful little chap.

> —*Remark to journalist and friend Noah Brooks, early*
> *December 1864*

ও

I can not frame a toast to Burns. I can say nothing worthy of his generous heart and transcending genius. Thinking of what he has said, I can not say anything which seems worth saying.

> —*Note to himself on being asked for a sentiment on the 106th birthday*
> *of the poet Robert Burns, January 25, 1865*

ও

SECESSION

We, the majority, would not strive to dissolve the Union; and if any attempt is made it must be you, who so loudly stigmatize us as disunionists. But the Union, in any event, won't be dissolved. We don't want to dissolve it, and if you attempt it, *we won't let you.* With the purse and the sword, the army and navy and treasury in our hands and at our command, you *couldn't do it.* This Government would be very weak, indeed, if a majority, with a disciplined army and navy, and a well-filled treasury, could not preserve itself when attacked by an unarmed, undisciplined, unorganized minority.

All this talk about the dissolution of the Union is humbug— nothing but folly. *We* won't dissolve the Union, and *you* shan't.

—*Speech, Galena, Illinois, July 23, 1856*

❧

Old John Brown has just been executed for treason against a state. We cannot object, even though he agreed with us in thinking slavery wrong. That cannot excuse violence, bloodshed, and treason. It could avail him nothing that he might think himself right. So, if constitutionally we elect a President, and therefore you undertake to destroy the Union, it will be our duty to deal with you as old John Brown has been dealt with. We shall try to do our duty. We hope and believe that in no section will a majority so act as to render such extreme measures necessary.

—*Speech, Leavenworth, Kansas, December 3, 1859*

❧

... you [the South] will not abide the election of a Republican President! In that supposed event, you say you will destroy the Union; and then you say the great crime of having destroyed it will be upon us! That is cool. A highwayman holds a pistol to my ear, and mutters through his teeth, "Stand and deliver, or I shall kill you, and then you will be a murderer!"

—*Speech, Cooper Union Institute, New York City,*
February 27, 1860

What is our present condition? We have just carried an election on principles fairly stated to the people. Now we are told in advance the government shall be broken up unless we surrender to those we have beaten before we take the offices. In this they are either attempting to play upon us, or they are in dead earnest. Either way, if we surrender, it is the end of us and of the government. They will repeat the experiment upon us *ad libitum*. A year will not pass till we shall have to take Cuba as a condition upon which they will stay in the Union.

—Letter to James Hale, January 11, 1861

The crisis, as it is called, is altogether an artificial crisis. In all parts of the nation there are differences of opinion and politics. ... Have they not all their rights now as they ever have had? Do they not have their fugitive slaves returned now as ever? Have they not the same constitution that they have lived under for seventy odd years? Have they not a position as citizens of this common country, and have we any power to change that position? What then is the matter with them? Why all this excitement? Why all these complaints? As I said before, this crisis is all artificial. It has no foundation in facts. It was not argued up, as the saying is, and cannot, therefore, be argued down. Let it alone and it will go down of itself.

—Speech at Cleveland, Ohio, February 15, 1861

If the minority will not acquiesce, the majority must, or the government must cease. There is no other alternative; for continuing the government is acquiescence on one side or the other. If a minority, in such a case, will secede rather than acquiesce, they make a precedent which, in turn, will divide and ruin them; for a minority of their own will secede from them, whenever a majority refuses to be controlled by such minority. For instance, why may not any portion of a new confederacy, a year or two hence, arbitrarily secede again, precisely as portions of the present Union now claim to secede from it. All who cherish disunion sentiments are now being educated to the exact temper of doing this. Is there such perfect identity of interests among the States to compose a new Union, as to produce harmony only, and prevent renewed secession?

—*First Inaugural Address, March 4, 1861*

ও

Physically speaking, we cannot separate. We cannot remove our respective sections from each other, nor build an impassable wall between them. A husband and wife may be divorced and go out of the presence, and beyond the reach of each other; but the different parts of our country cannot do this. They cannot but remain face to face; and intercourse, either amicable or hostile, must continue between them. Is it possible then to make that intercourse more advantageous, or more satisfactory, *after* separation than *before*? Can aliens make treaties easier than friends can make laws? Can treaties be more faithfully enforced between aliens than laws can among friends?

—*First inaugural address, March 4, 1861*

ও

I hold that in contemplation of universal law and of the Constitution, the Union of these States is perpetual. Perpetuity is implied, if not expressed, in the fundamental law of all national governments. It is safe to assert that no government proper ever had a provision in its organic law for its own termination. Continue to execute all the express provisions of our national Constitution, and the Union will endure forever—it being impossible to destroy it, except by some action not provided for in the instrument itself.

—*First inaugural address, March 4, 1861*

ও

That there are persons in one section or another who seek to destroy the Union at all events, and are glad of any pretext to do it, I will neither affirm or deny; but if there be such, I need address no word to them. To those, however, who really love the Union, may I not speak?

Before entering upon so grave a matter as the destruction of our national fabric, with all its benefits, its memories and hopes, would it not be wise to ascertain precisely why we do it? Will you hazard so desperate a step while there is any possibility that any portion of the ills you fly from have no real existence? Will you while the certain ills you fly to are greater than all the real ones you fly from? Will you risk the commission of so fearful a mistake?

—*First inaugural address, March 4, 1861*

ॐ

Plainly, the central idea of secession is the essence of anarchy. A majority, held in restraint by constitutional checks and limitations and always changing easily with deliberate changes of popular opinions and sentiments, is the only true sovereign of a free people. Whoever rejects it does, of necessity, fly to anarchy or to despotism. Unanimity is impossible; the rule of a minority, as a permanent arrangement, is wholly inadmissible; so that, rejecting the majority principle, anarchy or despotism in some form is all that is left.

—*First inaugural address, March 4, 1861*

ॐ

If it were admitted that you who are dissatisfied hold the right side in the dispute, there still is no single good reason for precipitate action. Intelligence, patriotism, Christianity, and a firm reliance on Him who has never yet forsaken this favored land are still competent to adjust, in the best way, all our present difficulty.

—*First inaugural address, March 4, 1861*

ॐ

In *your* hands, my dissatisfied fellow countrymen, and not in *mine*, is the momentous issue of civil war. The government will not assail *you*. You can have no conflict without being yourselves the aggressors. *You* have no oath registered in heaven to destroy the government, while *I* shall have the most solemn one to "preserve, protect and defend" it.

—*First inaugural address, March 4, 1861*

The States have their *status* in the Union, and they have no other *legal status*. If they break from this, they can only do so against law and by revolution. The Union, and not themselves separately, procured their independence and their liberty. By conquest, or purchase, the Union gave each of them whatever of independence and liberty it has.

—*Message to Congress in Special Session, July 4, 1861*

❧

Great honor is due to those officers who remained true, despite the example of their treacherous associates; but the greatest honor, and most important fact of all, is the unanimous firmness of the common soldiers and common sailors. To the last man, so far as is known, they have successfully resisted the traitorous efforts of those whose commands, but an hour before, they obeyed as absolute law. This is the patriotic instinct of plain people. They understand, without an argument, that destroying the Government which was made by Washington means no good to them.

—*Message to Congress in Special Session, July 4, 1861*

❧

It might seem, at first thought, to be of little difference whether the present movement at the South be called "secession" or "rebellion." The movers, however, well understand the difference. At the beginning they knew they could never raise their treason to any respectable magnitude by any name which implies *violation* of law. They knew their people possessed as much of moral sense, as much of devotion to law and order, and as much pride in and reverence for the history and government of their common country as any other civilized and patriotic people. They knew they could make no advancement directly in the teeth of these strong and noble sentiments. Accordingly, they commenced by an insidious debauching of the public mind. They invented an ingenious sophism which, if conceded, was followed by perfectly logical steps, through all the incidents, to the complete destruction of the Union. The sophism itself is that any State of the Union may *consistently* with the National Constitution, and therefore *lawfully* and *peacefully*, withdraw from the Union without the consent of the Union or of

any other State. The little disguise that the supposed right is to be exercised only for just cause, themselves to be the sole judges of its justice, is too thin to merit any notice.
—*Message to Congress in Special Session, July 4, 1861*

෨

Our States have neither more nor less power than that reserved to them in the Union by the Constitution—no one of them ever having been a State *out* of the Union. The original ones passed into the Union even *before* they cast off their British colonial dependence.
—*Message to Congress in Special Session, July 4, 1861*

෨

Much is said about the "sovereignty" of the States; but the word even is not in the National Constitution, nor, as is believed, in any of the State constitutions. What is "sovereignty" in the political sense of the term? Would it be far wrong to define it "a political community without a political superior"? Tested by this, no one of our States except Texas ever was a sovereignty. And even Texas gave up the character on coming into the Union; by which act she acknowledged the Constitution of the United States, and the laws and treaties of the United States made in pursuance of the Constitution, to be for her the supreme law of the land.
—*Message to Congress in Special Session, July 4, 1861*

෨

I most cordially sympathize with your Excellency in the wish to preserve the peace of my own native State, Kentucky; but it is with regret I search, and cannot find, in your not very short letter, any declaration, or intimation, that you entertain any desire for the preservation of the Federal Union.
—*Letter to Governor of Kentucky Beriah Magoffin,*
August 24, 1861

෨

I think to lose Kentucky is nearly the same as to lose the whole game. Kentucky gone, we can not hold Missouri, nor, as I think,

Maryland. These all against us, and the job on our hands is too large for us. We would as well consent to separation at once, including the surrender of this capitol.

—*Letter to Orville Browning, September 22, 1861*

శ

The right of a State to secede is not an open or debatable question.

—*Remark to his secretary John Nicolay, December 13, 1861*

శ

The people of Louisiana—all intelligent people everywhere— know full well that I never had a wish to touch the foundations of their society or any right of theirs. With perfect knowledge of this they forced a necessity upon me to send armies among them, and it is their own fault, not mine, that they are annoyed by the presence of General Phelps. They also know the remedy; know how to be cured of General Phelps. Remove the necessity of his presence. And might it not be well for them to consider whether they have not already had *time* enough to do this? If they can conceive of anything worse than General Phelps within my power, would they not better be looking out for it! They very well know the way to avert all this is simply to take their place in the Union upon the old terms. If they will not do this should they not receive harder blows rather than lighter ones?

—*Letter to Reverdy Johnson, July 26, 1862*

శ

Broken eggs cannot be mended; but Louisiana has nothing to do now but to take her place in the Union as it was, barring the already broken eggs. The sooner she does so, the smaller will be the amount of that which will be past mending. This government cannot much longer play a game in which it stakes all, and its enemies stake nothing. Those enemies must understand that they cannot experiment for ten years trying to destroy the government, and if they fail, still come back into the Union unhurt. If they expect in any contingency to ever have the Union as it was, I join with the writer in saying, "Now is the time."

—*Letter to August Belmont, July 31, 1862*

The division of a State is dreaded as a precedent. But a measure made expedient by a war is no precedent for times of peace. It is said that the admission of West Virginia is secession, and tolerated only because it is our secession. Well, if we call it by that name, there is still difference enough between secession against the Constitution, and secession in favor of the Constitution.

—Draft opinion on the admission of West Virginia into the Union,
c. December 31, 1862

Prior to my installation here it had been inculcated that any State had a lawful right to secede from the national Union; and that it would be expedient to exercise the right, whenever the devotees of the doctrine should fail to elect a President to their own liking. I was elected contrary to their liking; and accordingly, so far as it was legally possible, they had taken seven states out of the Union, had seized many of the United States Forts, and had fired upon the United States' Flag, all before I was inaugurated; and, of course, before I had done any official act whatever. The rebellion, thus began soon ran into the present civil war; and, in certain respects, it began on very unequal terms between the parties. The insurgents had been preparing for it more than thirty years, while the government had taken no steps to resist them.

—Letter to Erastus Corning and others on the arrest of the
"Copperhead" Clement L. Vallandigham, June 12, 1863

We all agree that the seceded States, so called, are out of their proper practical relation with the Union; and that the sole object of the government, civil and military, in regard to those States, is to again get them into that proper practical relation. I believe it is not only possible, but in fact easier to do this, without deciding, or even considering, whether these States have ever been out of the Union than with it.

—Last speech, from a White House balcony, April 11, 1865

Concede that the new government of Louisiana is only what it should be as the egg is to the fowl, we shall sooner have the fowl by hatching the egg than by smashing it.

—*Speech, Washington, D.C., April 11, 1865*

Slavery, Equality, and the Emancipation Proclamation

Pharaoh's country was cursed with plagues, and his hosts were drowned in the Red Sea for striving to retain a captive people who had already served them more than four hundred years. May like disasters never befall us!

—*Eulogy on Henry Clay, the State House, Springfield, Illinois, July 6, 1852*

The slavery question often bothered me as far back as 1836–40. I was troubled and grieved over it; but after the annexation of Texas I gave it up, believing as I now do, that God will settle it, and settle it right, and that he will, in some inscrutable way, restrict the spread of so great an evil; but for the present it is our duty to wait.

—*Remark to Robert H. Browne, early 1854*

If the negro is a *man*, why then my ancient faith teaches me that "all men are created equal"; and that there can be no moral right in connection with one man's making a slave of another.

—*Speech, Peoria, Illinois, October 16, 1854*

What *natural* right required Kansas and Nebraska to be opened to slavery? Is not slavery universally granted to be, in the abstract, a gross outrage on the law of nature? Have not all civilized nations, our own among them, made the slave trade capital, and classed it with piracy and murder? Is it not held to be the great wrong of the world? Do not the Southern people, the slaveholders themselves, spurn the domestic slave dealer, refuse to associate with him, or let their families associate with his family as long as the taint of his infamous calling is known?

—Speech, Springfield, Illinois, October 4, 1854

❧

… let me say that I think I have no prejudice against the Southern people. They are just what we would be in their situation. If slavery did not now exist amongst them, they would not introduce it. If it did now exist amongst us, we should not instantly give it up.—this I believe of the masses north and south.

—Speech, Peoria, Illinois, October 16, 1854

❧

Slavery is founded in the selfishness of man's nature—opposition to it is his love of justice.

—Speech, Peoria, Illinois, October 16, 1854

❧

Near eighty years ago we began by declaring that all men are created equal; but now from that beginning we have run down to the other declaration, that for *some* men to enslave others is a "sacred right of self-government." These principles can not stand together. They are as opposite as God and Mammon; and whoever holds to the one must despise the other.

—Speech, Peoria, Illinois, October 16, 1854

❧

So far as peaceful, voluntary emancipation is concerned, the condition of the negro slave in America, scarcely less terrible to the contemplation of a free mind, is now as fixed and hopeless of change for the better as that of the lost souls of the finally impenitent. The Autocrat of all the Russias will resign his crown and proclaim his subjects free republicans sooner than will our American masters voluntarily give up their slaves.

—Letter to George Robertson, August 15, 1855

ಀ

On the question of liberty, as a principle, we are not what we have been. When we were the political slaves of King George and wanted to be free, we called the maxim that "all men are created equal" a self-evident truth; but now when we have grown fat, and have lost all dread of being slaves ourselves, we have become so greedy to be *masters* that we call the same maxim "a self-evident lie."

—Letter to George Robertson, August 15, 1855

ಀ

Our progress in degeneracy appears to me to be pretty rapid. As a nation, we began by declaring that "all men *are created equal*." We now practically read it "all men are created equal, except *negroes*." … When it comes to this I should prefer emigrating to some country where they make no pretense of loving liberty—to Russia, for instance, where despotism can be taken pure, and without the base alloy of hypocrisy.

—Letter to his friend Joshua Speed, August 24, 1855

ಀ

I have noticed in Southern newspapers, particularly the Richmond *Enquirer*, the Southern view of the Free States. They insist that slavery has a right to spread. They defend it upon principle. They insist that their slaves are far better off than Northern freemen. What a mistaken view do these men have of Northern laborers! They think that men are always to remain laborers here—but there is no such class. The men who labored for another last year, this year labors for himself, and next year he will hire others to labor for him. These men don't understand when they think in this manner of Northern free labor.

—Speech, Kalamazoo, Michigan, August 27, 1856

The question of slavery, at the present day, should be not only the greatest question, but very nearly the sole question.

—Speech, Kalamazoo, Michigan, August 27, 1856

❧

My friends, we know that slavery is not right. If it were right, some men would have been born with no hands and two mouths, for it was designed that they should not work, but only eat. Other men would have been born with no mouth and four hands, because it was the design of the Creator that they should work that other men might eat. We are all born with a mouth to eat and hands to work, that every man may eat the products of his own labor and be satisfied.

*—Remark to his friend the clergyman Julian M. Sturtevant,
early September 1856*

❧

The assertion that "all men are created equal" was of no practical use in effecting our separation from Great Britain; and it was placed in the Declaration not for that, but for future use. Its authors meant it to be, thank God, it is now proving itself a stumbling block to those who in after times might seek to turn a free people back into the hateful paths of despotism.

—Speech at Springfield, June 26, 1857

❧

You will find that all the arguments in favor of king-craft were of this class; they always bestrode the necks of the people, not that they wanted to do it, but because the people were better off for being ridden. That is their argument, and this argument of the Judge [Stephen Douglas] is the same old serpent that says you work and I eat, you toil and I will enjoy the fruits of it. Turn it whatever way you will—whether it come from the mouth of a King an excuse for enslaving the people of his country, or from the mouth of men of one race as a reason for enslaving the men of another race, it is all the same old serpent, and I hold if that course of argumentation that is made for the purpose of convincing the public mind that we should not care about this should be granted, it does not stop with the negro. I should like to know if taking this old Declaration of Independence, which declares that all men are equal upon principle, and making exceptions to it, where will it stop? If one man says it does not mean a negro, why not another say it does not mean some other man?

—Speech, Chicago, July 10, 1858

❧

I have always hated slavery, I think, as much as any Abolitionist. I have been an Old Line Whig. I have always hated it, but I have always been quiet about it until this new era of the introduction of the Nebraska bill began. I always believed that everybody was against it, and it was in course of ultimate extinction.

—Speech, Chicago, July 10, 1858

❧

I have said I do not understand the Declaration to mean that all men were created equal in all respects. They are not our equal in color; but I suppose that it does mean to declare that all men are equal in some respects; they are equal in their right to "life, liberty and the pursuit of happiness." ... All I ask for the negro is that if you do not like him, let him alone.

—Speech, Chicago, July 10, 1858

❧

As I would not be a *slave*, so I would not be a *master*. This expresses my idea of democracy. Whatever differs from this, to the extent of the difference, is not democracy.

—Note, c. August 1858

❧

I leave it to you to say whether throughout the history of our government, from time to time, has not this institution of slavery always failed to be a bond of union, but on the contrary, proved to be an apple of discord, and an element of discord, in the house, and

I ask you to consider whether so long as the structure of men's minds shall continue as God has seen fit to make them, this question of slavery will not continue to be an element of discord in the houses.

—*Debate reply to Stephen Douglas, Ottawa, Illinois, August 21, 1858*

❧

... there is no reason in the world why the negro is not entitled to all the natural rights enumerated in the Declaration of Independence, the right to life, liberty and the pursuit of happiness.

—*First debate with Stephen Douglas, Ottawa, Illinois,*
August 21, 1858

❧

Slavery is not a matter of little importance: it overshadows every other question in which we are interested. It has divided the Methodist and Presbyterian churches, and has sown discord in the American Tract Society. The churches have split, and the Society will follow their example before long. So it will be seen that slavery is agitated in the religious as well as in the political world.

—*Speech, Clinton, Illinois, September 2, 1858*

❧

What constitutes the bulwark of our own liberty and independence? ... Our reliance is in the love of liberty which God has planted in our bosoms. Our defense is in the preservation of the spirit which prizes liberty as the heritage of all men, in all lands, everywhere. Destroy this spirit, and you have planted the seeds of despotism around your own doors.

—*Speech, Edwardsville, Illinois, September 11, 1858*

❧

Suppose it is true that the negro is inferior to the white in the gifts of nature; is it not the exact reverse justice that the white should, for that reason, take from the negro any part of the little which has been given him? "*Give* to him that is needy" is the Christian rule of charity; but "Take from him that is needy" is the rule of slavery.

—Note, c. October 1, 1858

&

As a good thing, slavery is strikingly peculiar, in this, that it is the only good thing which no man ever seeks the good of *for himself!*

Nonsense! Wolves devouring lambs, not because it is good for their own greedy maws, but because it is good for the lambs!

—Note, c. October 1, 1858

&

... while Mr. Jefferson was the owner of slaves, as he undoubtedly was, he, speaking on this very subject, used the strong language that he trembled for his country, when he remembered that God was just.

—Debate with Stephen Douglas, reply, Galesburg, Illinois,
October 7, 1858

&

Every thought that he utters will be seen to exclude the thought that there is anything wrong in slavery. You will take his speeches and get the short pointed sentiments expressed by him, that he does not care if slavery is voted up, or voted down, and such like, you will see at once it is a perfectly logical idea if you admit that slavery is not wrong, but if it is wrong, Judge Douglas cannot say that he don't care for a wrong being voted up. Judge Douglas declares that if any community wants slavery they can have it. He can logically say that, if he admits that there is no wrong in it, but he cannot say that, if he admits that there is wrong in it.

—Debate with Stephen Douglas, reply, Galesburg, Illinois,
October 7, 1858

&

... what has ever threatened our own liberties and prosperity save and except this very institution of slavery? If this be true, how do you propose to amend it? By spreading it out larger, or making it bigger? You may have a cancer upon your person, and you may not be able to cut it out at once, lest you bleed to death, but you may not treat it as a wrong by spreading it over your whole body. So with this, the way is—is the peaceful mode to deal with it—to prevent the spread of it into new country. That is the old fashioned way of dealing with it, the example which our fathers have set us.

> —*Debate with Stephen Douglas, reply, Alton, Illinois,*
> *October 15, 1858*

❧

These are the two principles that are made the eternal struggle between right and wrong. They are the two principles that have stood face to face, one of them asserting the divine right of kings, the same principle that says you work, you toil, you earn bread, and I will eat it. It is the same old serpent, whether it come from the mouth of a king who seeks to bestride the people of his nation, and to live upon the fat of his neighbor, or, whether it comes from one race of men as an apology for the enslaving of another race of men.

> —*Debate with Stephen Douglas, reply, Alton, Illinois,*
> *October 15, 1858*

❧

This is a world of compensations; and he who would be no slave must consent to have no slave. Those who deny freedom to others deserve it not for themselves; and, under a just God, cannot long retain it.

> —*Letter to H. L. Pierce and others, April 6, 1859*

❧

We want, and must have, a national policy as to slavery which deals with it as being a wrong.

> —*Notes for his speeches at Columbus and Cincinnati, Ohio,*
> *September 16–17, 1859*

Slavery is doomed, and that within a few years. Even Judge Douglas admits it to be an evil, and an evil can't stand discussion. In discussing it, we have taught a great many thousands of people to hate it who had never given it a thought before. What kills the skunk is the publicity it gives itself. What a skunk wants to do is to keep snug under the barn in the daytime, when men are around with shotguns.

—*Remark to the author David Ross Locke (a.k.a. Petroleum V. Nasby), September 16, 1859*

❧

… we know from Judge Douglas himself that slavery began to be an element of discord among the white people of this country as far back as 1699, or one hundred and sixty years ago, or five generations of men—counting thirty years to a generation. Now it would seem to me that it might have occurred to Judge Douglas, or anybody who had turned his attention to these facts, that there was something in the nature of that thing, slavery, somewhat durable for mischief and discord.

—*Speech, Columbus, Ohio, September 16, 1859*

❧

He [Thomas Jefferson] supposed there was a question of God's eternal justice wrapped up in the enslaving of any race of men, or any man, and that those who did so braved the arm of Jehovah—that when a nation thus dared the Almighty every friend of that nation had cause to dread His wrath. Choose ye between Jefferson and Douglas as to what is the true view of this element among us.

—*Speech, Columbus, Ohio, September 16, 1859*

❧

Free labor has the inspiration of hope; pure slavery has no hope. The power of hope upon human exertion and happiness is wonderful.

—*Note on labor, c. September 17, 1859*

I always thought that the man who made the corn should eat the corn.
—*Remark to Cassius M. Clay, who would become Lincoln's Minister to Russia, 1860*

ço

One section of our country believes slavery is *right*, and ought to be extended, while the other believes it is *wrong*, and ought not to be extended. This is the only substantial dispute.
—*First Inaugural Address, March 4, 1861*

ço

I beseech you to make the arguments for yourselves. You can not, if you would, be blind to the signs of the times.
—*Proclamation overruling General David Hunter's orders emancipating the slaves in Georgia, Florida and South Carolina, but asking the border states to begin measures for abolition, May 19, 1862*

ço

Gentlemen, this American slavery is no small affair, and it cannot be done away with at once. It is a part of our national life. It is not of yesterday. It began in colonial times. In one way or another it has shaped nearly everything that enters into what we call government. It is as much northern as it is southern. It is not merely a local or geographical institution. It belongs to our politics, to our industries, to our commerce, and to our religion. Every portion of our territory in some form or another has contributed to the growth and the increase of slavery. It has been nearly two hundred years coming up to its present proportions. It is wrong, a great evil indeed, but the South is no more responsible for the wrong done to the African race than is the North.
—*Remark to the clergyman Elbert Porter, July 1862*

ço

We must free the slaves or be ourselves subdued. The slaves were undeniably an element of strength to those who had their service, and we must decide whether that element should be with us or against us.

—*Remark to Secretary of the Navy Gideon Welles, July 13, 1862. (On July 22, Lincoln broached to his cabinet his intention to issue an emancipation proclamation.)*

❧

Had slavery no existence among us, and were the question asked shall we adopt such an institution, we should agree as to the reply which should be made. If there be any diversity in our views it is not as to whether we should receive slavery when free from it, but as to how we may best get rid of it already amongst us. Were an individual asked whether he would wish to have a wen on his neck, he could not hesitate as to the reply; but were it asked whether a man who has such a wen should at once be relieved of it by the application of a surgeon's knife, there might be diversity of opinion, perhaps the man might bleed to death as the result of such an operation.

—*Speech to a committee from the Synod of the Reformed Presbyterian Church, July 17, 1862*

❧

Would my word free the slaves, when I cannot even enforce the Constitution in the rebel states?

—*Remark to a group of ministers from Chicago, September 13, 1862*

❧

What good would a proclamation of emancipation from me do, especially as we are now situated? I do not want to issue a document that the whole world will see must necessarily be inoperative, like the Pope's bull against the comet!

—*Remark to a group of ministers from Chicago, September 13, 1862*

❧

It is my earnest desire to know the will of Providence in this matter [of emancipation]. *And if I can learn what it is I will do it!*

—*Remark to a group of ministers from Chicago, September 13, 1862*

When the rebel army was at Frederick, I determined, as soon as it should be driven out of Maryland, to issue a proclamation of emancipation, such as I thought most likely to be useful. I said nothing to anyone; but I made the promise to myself and to my Maker. The rebel army is now driven out, and I am going to fulfill that promise.

—*Remark to his cabinet, September 22, 1862*

❧

I have, as you are aware, thought a great deal about the relation of this war to slavery; and you all remember that, several weeks ago, I read to you an order I had prepared on this subject, which, on account of objections made by some of you, was not issued. Ever since then, my mind has been much occupied with this subject, and I have thought all along that the time for acting on it might very probably come. I think the time has come now. I wish it were a better time. I wish that we were in a better condition. The action of the army against the rebels has not been quite what I should have best liked. But they have been driven out of Maryland, and Pennsylvania is no longer in danger of invasion.

—*Remark to his cabinet on the Preliminary Emancipation Proclamation, September 22, 1862*

❧

I have got you together to hear what I have written down. I do not wish your advice about the main matter; for that I have determined for myself. This I say without intending anything but respect for any one of you. But I already know the views of each on this question. They have been heretofore expressed, and I have considered them as thoroughly and carefully as I can. What I have written is that which my reflections have determined me to say. If there is anything in the expressions I use, or in any other minor matter, which any one of you thinks had best be changed, I shall be glad to receive the suggestions.

—*Remark to his cabinet on the Preliminary Emancipation Proclamation, September 22, 1862*

... on the first day of January in the year of our Lord, one thousand eight hundred and sixty-three, all persons held as slaves within any state, or designated part of a state, the people whereof shall then be in rebellion against the United States, shall be then, thenceforward, and forever free ...

—Preliminary Emancipation Proclamation, September 22, 1862

❧

I can only trust in God I have made no mistake.

—Remark to an enthusiastic crowd at the Executive Mansion on his making the preliminary Emancipation Proclamation, September 24, 1862

❧

The North responds to the proclamation sufficiently in breath, but breath alone kills no rebels.

—Letter to Vice President Hannibal Hamlin, September 28, 1862

❧

Without slavery the rebellion could never have existed; without slavery it could not continue.

—Annual Message to Congress, December 1, 1862

❧

I never in my life felt more certain that I was doing right than I do in signing this paper. But I have been receiving calls and shaking hands since nine o'clock this morning till my arm is stiff and numb. Now, this signature is one that will be closely examined, and if they find my hand trembled, they will say, "He had some compunctions." But, anyway, it is going to be done.

—Remark on signing the Emancipation Proclamation, January 1, 1863

❧

Now, therefore I, Abraham Lincoln, President of the United States, by virtue of the power in me vested as Commander-in-Chief, of the Army and Navy of the United States in time of actual armed rebellion against the authority and government of the United States, and as a fit and necessary war measure for suppressing said rebellion, do, on this first day of January, in the year of our Lord one thousand eight hundred and sixty-three, and in accordance with my purpose so to do publicly proclaimed for the full period of one hundred days, from the day first above mentioned, order and designate as the States and parts of States wherein the people thereof respectively, are this day in rebellion against the United States, the following, to wit ...

... that all persons held as slaves within said designated States, and parts of States, are, and henceforward shall be free; and that the Executive government of the United States, including the military and naval authorities thereof, will recognize and maintain the freedom of said persons.

—*Final Emancipation Proclamation, January 1, 1863*

After the commencement of hostilities I struggled nearly a year and a half to get along without touching the "institution"; and when finally I conditionally determined to touch it, I gave a hundred days' fair notice of my purpose, to all the States and people, within which time they could have turned it wholly aside, by simply again becoming good citizens of the United States. They chose to disregard it, and I made the peremptory proclamation on what appeared to me to be a military necessity. And being made, it must stand.

—*Letter to General John A. McClernand, January 8, 1863*

The resources, advantages, and powers of the American people are very great, and they have, consequently, succeeded to equally great responsibilities. It seems to have devolved upon them to test whether a government established on the principles of human freedom can be maintained against an effort to build one upon the exclusive foundation of human bondage.

—*Letter to the Workingmen of London, February 2, 1863*

The colored population is the great *available* and yet *unavailed of* force for restoring the Union. The bare sight of fifty thousand armed and drilled black soldiers on the banks of the Mississippi would end the rebellion at once.

—*Letter to Governor of Tennessee Andrew Johnson, March 26, 1863*

❧

To sell or enslave any captured person, on account of his color, and for no offence against the laws of war, is a relapse into barbarism and a crime against the civilization of the age. ...

It is therefore ordered that for every soldier of the United States killed in violation of the laws of war, a rebel soldier shall be executed; and for everyone enslaved by the enemy or sold into slavery, a rebel soldier shall be placed at hard labor on the public works and continued at such labor until the other shall be released and receive the treatment due to a prisoner of war.

—*General Orders, Number 252, July 31, 1863*

❧

Now, as to pay, we had to make some concessions to prejudice. There were threats that if we made soldiers of them at all, white men would not enlist, would not fight beside them. Besides, it was not believed that a Negro could make a good soldier, as good a soldier as a white man, and hence it was thought that he should not have the same pay as a white man. But I assure you, Mr. Douglass, that in the end they shall have the same pay as white soldiers.

—*Remark to Frederick Douglass on the enlistment of black soldiers,*
August 10, 1863

❧

You say you will not fight to free negroes. Some of them seem willing to fight for you; but, no matter. Fight you, then, exclusively to save the Union. I issued the proclamation on purpose to aid you in saving the Union.

—*Letter to James C. Conkling of Illinois, August 26, 1863*

… the proclamation, as law, either is valid, or is not valid. If it is not valid, it needs no retraction. If it is valid, it cannot be redacted any more than the dead can be brought to life.
—*Letter to James C. Conkling of Illinois, August 26, 1863*

୬

It was a somewhat remarkable fact that there were just one hundred days between the dates of the two proclamations, issued upon the 22nd of September and the 1st of January. I had not made the calculation at the time.
—*Remark to his portrait painter, Francis B. Carpenter, February 6, 1864*

୬

If slavery is not wrong, nothing is wrong.
—*Remark to Kentucky Governor Thomas Bramlette,*
Frankfort Commonwealth *editor Albert Hodges,*
and Senator Archibald Dixon, March 26, 1864

୬

The world has never had a good definition of the word liberty, and the American people, just now, are much in want of one. We all declare for liberty; but in using the same *word* we do not all mean the same *thing*. With some the word liberty may mean for each man to do as he pleases with himself, and the product of his labor; while with others the same word may mean for some men to do as they please with other men, and the product of other men's labor. Here are two, not only different, but incompatible things, called by the same name—liberty. And it follows that each of the things is, by the respective parties, called by two different and incompatible names—liberty and tyranny.
—*Speech, Sanitary Fair, Baltimore, Maryland, April 18, 1864*

୬

I expect you have reference to my having emancipated the slaves in my proclamation. But [mentioning Washington and several other presidents] they were all just as good, and would have done just as I had done if the time had come. If the people over the river [pointing across the Potomac] had behaved themselves, I could not have done what I have, but they did not, and I was compelled to do these things.

—Remark to the abolitionist and former slave Sojourner Truth,
October 29, 1864

ço

... if it was wrong in the South to hold slaves, it was wrong in the North to carry on the slave trade and sell them to the South.

—Remark to Secretary of State William H. Seward,
February 3, 1865

ço

If we shall suppose that American slavery is one of those offenses which, in the providence of God, must needs come, but which, having continued through His appointed time, He now wills to remove, and that He gives to both North and South this terrible war as the woe due to those by whom the offence came, shall we discern therein any departure from those divine attributes which the believers in a living God always ascribe to Him?

—Second Inaugural Address, March 4, 1865

ço

I have in my lifetime heard many arguments why the negroes ought to be slaves; but if they fight for those who would keep them in slavery it will be a better argument than any I have yet heard. He who will fight for that ought to be a slave. ... While I have often said that all men ought to be free, yet I would allow those colored persons to be slaves who want to be; and next to them those white persons who argue in favor of making other people slaves. I am in favor of giving an opportunity to such white men to try it on themselves.

—Speech to the 140th Indiana Regiment, on the Confederate Army's
plan to enlist slaves, March 17, 1865

A man who denies to other men equality of rights is hardly worthy of freedom; but I would give even to him all the rights which I claim for myself.

—*Remark to his assistant private secretary John Hay,*
April 1865

❧

SPEECH-MAKING

Extemporaneous speaking should be practiced and cultivated. It is the lawyer's avenue to the public. However able and faithful he may be in other respects, people are slow to bring him business if he cannot make a speech. And yet there is not a more fatal error to young lawyers than relying too much on speech-making. If anyone, upon his rare powers of speaking, shall claim an exemption from the drudgery of the law, his case is a failure in advance.

—*Notes for a lecture on law, c. July 1850*

❧

Try to think they're your own words and talk them as you would talk them to me.

—*Remark on public-speaking to a Springfield boy,*
John Langdon Kaine, c. 1850s

❧

Billy, don't shoot too high; shoot low down, and the common people will understand you. They are the ones which you wish to reach; at least, they are the ones whom you ought to reach. The educated ones will understand you anyhow. If you shoot too high, your bullets go over the heads of the mass and only hit those who need no hitting.

—*Remark to William H. Herndon, Lincoln's law partner*
in Springfield, Illinois (n.d.)

I am compelled by nature to speak slowly. I commence way back like the boys do when they want to get a good start. My weight and speed get momentum to jump far.

—Remark to William H. Herndon (n.d.)

✎

Look here, my friend, you are only making a fool of yourself by exposing yourself to the ridicule which I have thus far succeeded in bringing upon you every time you have interrupted me. You ought to know that men whose business it is to speak in public make it a part of their business to have something always ready for just such fellows as you are. You see you stand no show against a man who has met, a hundred times, just such flings as you seem to fancy are original with yourself; so you may as well, to use a popular expression, "dry up" at once.

—Remark to a heckler during a campaign speech for John C. Fremont, the Republican nominee for president, July 17, 1856

✎

I do wish it was through. When I have to speak, I always feel nervous till I get well into it. ... I hide it as well as I can, but it's just as I tell you.

—Remark to an Illinois acquaintance, 1856

✎

Gentlemen, reading from speeches is a very tedious business, particularly for an old man that has to put on spectacles, and the more so if the man be so tall that he has to bend over to the light.

—Speech, Chicago, July 10, 1858

✎

You don't know what you are talking about, my friend. I am quite willing to answer any gentleman in the crowd who asks an *intelligent* question.

—Answering a heckler during a speech in Chicago, July 10, 1858

Gentlemen, Judge Douglas informed you that this speech of mine was probably carefully prepared. I admit that it was. I am not master of language; I have not a fine education; I am not capable of entering into a disquisition upon dialectics, as I believe you call it; but I do not believe the language I employed bears any such construction as Judge Douglas put upon it. But I don't care about a quibble in regard to words. I know what I meant, and I will not leave this crowd in doubt, if I can explain it to them, what I really meant in the use of that paragraph.

—Speech, Chicago, July 10, 1858

ତ

Well, Tom, if you have a nice little speech all ready, you may deliver it, but if not, I would a great deal rather have the time.

—Remark to Thomas J. Henderson, a Toulon, Illinois, lawyer
and legislator, Fall 1858

ତ

John, it depends a great deal on how you state a case. When Daniel Webster stated a case, it was half-argument. No, you take the subject of predestination; you state it one way, and you cannot make much of it; you state it another, and it seems quite reasonable.

—Remark to John Littlefield, a law student of Lincoln and his partner
William Herndon, c. 1859–1860

ତ

You know that it has not been my custom, since I started on the route to Washington, to make long speeches; I am rather inclined to silence, and whether that be wise or not, it is at least more unusual nowadays to find a man who can hold his tongue than to find one who cannot.

—Speech, Monongahela House, Pittsburgh, Pennsylvania,
February 14, 1861

I have made a great many poor speeches in my life, and I feel considerably relieved now to know that the dignity of the position in which I have been placed does not permit me to expose myself any longer. I therefore take shelter, most gladly, in standing back and allowing you to hear speeches from gentlemen who are so very much more able to make them than myself. I thank you for the kindness of your call, but I must keep my word, and not be led into a speech, as I told you I did not appear for that purpose.

—*Remarks to New York regiments, Washington, D.C.,*
July 4, 1861

৬৹

The Secretary of War, you know, holds a pretty tight rein on the Press, so that they shall not tell more than they ought to, and I'm afraid that if I blab too much, he might draw a tight rein on me.

—*Speech, Jersey City, New Jersey, at a rail stop while returning to*
Washington, D.C., from West Point, June 24, 1862

৬৹

It was very kind in Mr. Everett to send me this. I suppose he was afraid I should say something that he wanted to say. He needn't have been alarmed. My speech isn't long.

—*Remark to journalist and friend Noah Brooks, on Edward Everett's*
Gettysburg address, November 14, 1863

৬৹

In my position it is somewhat important that I should not say any foolish things.

A Voice: If you can help it.

Mr. Lincoln: It very often happens that the only way to help it is to say nothing at all.

Believing that is my present condition this evening, I must beg of you to excuse me from addressing you.

—*Remarks to his "fellow-citizens" at Gettysburg, Pennsylvania,*
the day before his Gettysburg Address, November 18, 1863

I am glad to see you. I saw you in the crowd today, listening to my inaugural address; how did you like it? ... there is no man in the country whose opinion I value more than yours.

 —*Remark to Frederick Douglass, March 4, 1865 (Douglass answered, "Mr. Lincoln, that was a sacred effort.")*

❧

I expect it to wear as well as—perhaps better than—anything I have produced; but I believe it is not immediately popular. Men are not flattered by being shown that there has been a difference of purpose between the Almighty and them. To deny it, however, in this case, is to deny that there is a God governing the world. It is a truth which I thought needed to be told; and as whatever of humiliation there is in it falls most directly on myself, I thought others might afford for me to tell it.

 —*Letter to Thurlow Weed, on the reception of Lincoln's second inaugural address, March 15, 1865*

❧

STORYTELLING

If it were not for these stories, jokes, jests, I should die; they give vent—are the vents—of my moods and gloom.

 —*Remark to William H. Herndon, Lincoln's law partner in Springfield, Illinois (n.d.)*

❧

There was a man who was to be nominated at a political convention and hired a horse of a livery keeper to journey there. The horse was so confoundedly slow, however, that the man arrived too late, and found his opponent nominated and the convention adjourned. When he arrived home he said to the stableman, "This is a fine animal of yours—a fine animal." "Do you think so?" "Certainly, but never sell him to an undertaker." "Undertaker! Why not?" "Because if the horse were hitched to a hearse, resurrection day would come before he reached the cemetery." So if my journey goes on at this slow rate it will be resurrection day before I reach the capital.

—Anecdote recounted to a crowd at a station stop on his train to Washington, D.C., February 1861

I do generally remember a good story when I hear it, but I never did invent anything original; I am only a retail dealer.

—Remark to journalist and friend Noah Brooks (early 1860s)

They say I tell a great many stories. I reckon I do, but I have found in the course of a long experience that common people take them as they run, are more easily influenced and informed through the medium of a broad illustration than in any other way, and as to what the hypercritical few may think, I don't care. … I have originated but two stories in my life, but I tell tolerably well other people's stories.

—Remark to Chauncey Depew of New York, 1864

When quite young, at school, Daniel was one day guilty of a gross violation of the rules. He was detected in the act and called up by the teacher for punishment. This was to be the old-fashioned "feruling" of the hand. His hands happened to be very dirty. Knowing this, on his way to the teacher's desk he spit upon the palm of his right hand, wiping it off upon the side of his pantaloons. "Give me your hand, sir," said the teacher, very sternly. Out went the right hand, partly cleansed. The teacher looked at it a moment, and said, "Daniel, if you will find another hand in this schoolroom as filthy as that, I will let you off this time." Instantly from behind his back came the left hand. "Here it is, sir," was the ready reply. "That will do," said the teacher, "for this time; you can take your seat sir!"

—Anecdote, retelling a story about Daniel Webster, May 31, 1864

Well, there are two ways of relating a story. If you have an auditor who has the time and is inclined to listen, lengthen it out, pour it out slowly as if from a jug. If you have a poor listener, hasten it, shorten it, shoot it out of a popgun.

—*Remark to the pastor Phineas Gurney during the war*

&

THE WAR AND HIS GENERALS

The rebels attack Fort Sumter, and your citizens attack troops sent to the defense of the Government and the lives and property in Washington, and yet you would have me break my oath and surrender the Government without a blow. There is no Washington in that—no Jackson in that—no manhood nor honor in that.

—*Remarks to a YMCA committee from Baltimore,*
April 22, 1861

&

I intend at present, always leaving an opportunity for change of mind, to fill Fortress Monroe with men and stores, blockade the ports effectually, provide for the entire safety of the capital, keep them quietly employed in this way, and then go down to Charleston and pay her the little debt we are owing her.

—*Remark to his assistant private secretary John Hay,*
April 25, 1861

&

I have no desire to invade the South; but I must have troops to defend this Capital. Geographically [Washington] lies surrounded by the soil of Maryland; and mathematically the necessity exists that they should come over her territory. Our men are not moles, and can't dig under the earth; they are not birds, and can't fly through the air. There is no way but to march across, and that they must do. But in doing this there is no need of collision. Keep your rowdies in Baltimore, and there will be no bloodshed. Go home and tell your people that if they will not attack us, we will

not attack them; but if they do attack us, we will return it, and that severely.
>   —*Remarks to a YMCA committee from Baltimore, April 22, 1861*

ᏇᎣ

I will make no apology, gentlemen, for my weakness; but I knew poor Ellsworth well and held him in great regard. Just as you entered the room, Captain Fox left me, after giving me the painful details of Ellsworth's unfortunate death. The event was so unexpected, and the recital so touching, that it quite unmanned me. ... Poor fellow, it was undoubtedly an act of rashness, but it only shows the heroic spirit that animates our soldiers, from high to low, in this righteous cause of ours. Yet who can restrain their grief to see them fall in such a way as this, not by the fortunes of war, but by the hand of an assassin?
>   —*Remark to a newspaper reporter after having cried at the news of Colonel Elmer Ellsworth's death, May 25, 1861*

ᏇᎣ

You are green, it is true, but they are green, also; you are all green alike.
>   —*Remark to Brigadier General Irvin McDowell, on his battle plan for Manassas (Bull Run), June 29, 1861*

ᏇᎣ

The people of Virginia have thus allowed this giant insurrection to make its nest within her borders; and this government has no choice left but to deal with it *where* it finds it.
>   —*Message to Congress in Special Session, July 4, 1861*

ᏇᎣ

Gentlemen, my position in regard to your state is like that of the woodman, who, returning to his home one night, found coiled around his beautiful children, who were quietly sleeping in their bed, several poisonous snakes. His first impulse was to save his little ones, but he feared that if he struck at the snakes he might strike the children, and yet he dared not let them die without an effort.

So it is with me. I know Kentucky and Tennessee are infested with the enemies of the Union, but I know also that there are thousands of patriots in both who will be persecuted even unto death unless the strong hand of the government is interposed for their protection and rescue. We must go in. The old flag must be carried into Tennessee at whatever hazard.

—Remark to commissioners from Kentucky protesting the movement of Union troops, July 1861

❧

Doctor, although you do not know me, I know you. You are getting up a hospital for those who may fall sick or be wounded in the defense of the Union. I have been there and have seen you at work, although you were not aware of it. I want to aid you in your preparations for taking care of the poor fellows who will need all that we can do for them. When you need anything don't let there be any red tape. Come to me at once without hesitation, and you shall have anything you want if I can get it for you.

—Remark to a staff surgeon for the army, July 1861

❧

It has been said that one bad general is better than two good ones; and the saying is true, if taken to mean no more than that an army is better directed by a single mind, though inferior, than by two superior ones at variance and cross-purposes with each other. And the same is true in all joint operations wherein those engaged *can* have none but a common end in view, and *can* differ only as to the choice of means. In a storm at sea no one on board can wish the ship to sink; and yet not infrequently all go down together because too many will direct, and no single mind can be allowed to control.

—Annual Message to Congress, December 3, 1861

❧

"Act well your part, there all the honor lies." He who does *something* at the head of one regiment will eclipse him who does *nothing* at the head of a hundred.

—Letter to Major General David Hunter (Lincoln quotes the poet Alexander Pope), December 31, 1861

Delay is ruining us; and it is indispensable for me to have something definite.

—Telegram to General Henry W. Halleck, January 7, 1862

❧

… I state my general idea of this war to be that we have the *greater* numbers and the enemy has the *greater* facility of concentrating forces upon points of collision; that we must fail unless we can find some way of making our advantage an overmatch for *his*; and that this can only be done by menacing him with superior forces at *different* points at the *same* time, so that we can safely attack one or both if he makes no change; and if he *weakens* one to *strengthen* the other, forbear to attack the strengthened one, but seize and hold the weakened one, gaining so much.

—Letter to Brigadier General Don C. Buell, January 13, 1862

❧

Have you noticed the facts that less than one half-day's cost of this war would pay for all the slaves in Delaware, at four hundred dollars per head?—that eighty-seven days' cost of this war would pay for all in Delaware, Maryland, District of Columbia, Kentucky, and Missouri at the same price? Were those States to take the step, do you doubt that it would shorten the war more than eighty-seven days, and thus be an actual saving of expense. Please look at these things, and consider whether there should not be another article in the *Times*?

—Letter to Henry Raymond, March 9, 1862

❧

I expect to maintain this contest until successful, or till I die, or am conquered, or my term expires, or Congress or the country forsakes me; and I would publicly appeal to the country for this new force were it not that I fear a general panic and stampede would follow— so hard is it to have a thing understood as it really is. I think the new force should be all, or nearly all, infantry, principally because such can be raised most cheaply and quickly.

—Letter to Secretary of State William Steward, June 28, 1862

Sturgis, I cannot call to mind now any single event of my administration that gave me so much pain or wounded me so deeply as the singular behavior of Colonel Magruder on the very night before he abandoned us. ... He came to see me the very evening before he left and voluntarily said, while expressing his abhorrence of secession, "Sir, I was brought up and educated under the glorious old flag. I have lived under it and have fought under it, and, sir, with the help of God, I shall fight under it again and, if need be, shall die under it." The very next day, Magruder abandoned us, so that at the very moment he was making to me these protestations of loyalty and devotion, he must have had his mind fully made up to leave; and it seemed the more wanton and cruel in him because he knew that I had implicit confidence in his integrity. The fact is, when I learned that he had gone over to the enemy and I had been so completely deceived in him, my confidence was shaken in everybody, and I hardly knew who to trust any more.

—Remark to General Samuel D. Sturgis, Summer 1862

Sir, since the war began I have received a great deal of advice from all classes of men, and in the army great promises have been made, and my experience and observation has been that those who promise the most do the least.

—Remark to a man claiming that with a generalship he could defeat the Sioux in Minnesota, August 1862

I regard General Banks as one of the best men in the army. He makes me no trouble; but, with a large force or a small force, he always knows his duty and does it.

—Remark to a New York newspaper editor, August 12, 1862

Well, John, we are whipped again, I am afraid. The enemy reinforced on Pope and drove back his left wing, and he has retired to

Centreville, where he says he will be able to hold his men. I don't like that expression. I don't like to hear him admit that his men need "holding."

—*Remark to his assistant private secretary John Hay,*
August 31, 1862

ॐ

Doesn't it strike you as queer that I, who couldn't cut the head off of a chicken, and who was sick at the sight of blood, should be cast into the middle of a great war, with blood flowing all about me?

—*Remark to Congressman Daniel Voorhees of Indiana (n.d.)*

ॐ

Is this the man who wrote *The Decline and Fall of the Roman Empire*? ... Never mind, General, if you will write the decline and fall of this rebellion, I will let you off.

—*Remark to General John Gibbon, 1862*

ॐ

I sincerely wish war was an easier and pleasanter business than it is; but it does not admit of holidays.

—*Remark to Thomas H. Clay, asking for his army division's reassign-*
ment to Kentucky, c. September 1862

ॐ

So this is the little lady who made this big war?

—*Remark to the author of* Uncle Tom's Cabin, *Harriet Beecher*
Stowe, November 1862

ॐ

Whichever way it ends, I have the impression that I shan't last long after it's over.

—*Remark to author Harriet Beecher Stowe,*
November 1862

If there is a worse place than hell, I am in it.
>—*Remark to "a visitor," after the defeat at Fredericksburg,*
>*December 1862*

ဆ

We are now on the brink of destruction. It appears to me the Almighty is against us, and I can hardly see a ray of hope.
>—*Remark to Orville Browning, December 18, 1862, after the defeat at*
>*Fredericksburg*

ဆ

We are like whalers who have been on a long chase. We have at last got the harpoon into the monster, but we must look now how we steer, or with one flop of his tail he will send us all into eternity.
>—*Remark to New York Governor Edwin Morgan, January 1863*

ဆ

As to any dread of my having a "purpose to enslave, or exterminate, the whites of the South," I can scarcely believe that such dread exists. It is too absurd. I believe you can be my personal witness that no man is less to be dreaded for undue severity, in any case.
>—*Letter to General John A. McClernand,*
>*January 8, 1863*

ဆ

I fear neither you nor your officers appreciate the supreme importance to us of *time.* The more you prepare, the more the enemy will be prepared.
>—*Remark to Admiral Samuel F. Du Pont, March 20, 1863*

ဆ

I do not think the people of Pennsylvania should be uneasy about an invasion. Doubtless a small force of the enemy is flourishing about in the Northern part of Virginia on the "screw-horn" principle, on purpose to divert us in another quarter. I believe it is nothing more. We think we have adequate forces close after them.

—Letter to Governor Andrew Curtin of Pennsylvania, April 28, 1863
(Two months later the Confederates invaded southern Pennsylvania, and
the Union forces met and defeated them at Gettysburg.)

෧

Let your military measures be strong enough to repel the invader and keep the peace, and not so strong as to unnecessarily harass and persecute the people. It is a difficult role, and so much greater will be the honor if you perform it well.

—Letter to General John M. Schofield on his having assigned Schofield
to the command of the Department of the Missouri, May 17, 1863

෧

If General —— had known how big a funeral he would have had, he would have died years ago.

—Remark to David R. Locke ("Petroleum V. Nasby"),
humorist (n.d.)

෧

I think you do not know how embarrassing your request is. Few things are so troublesome to the government as the fierceness with which the profits of trading in cotton are sought. The temptation is so great that nearly every body wishes to be in it; and when in, the question of profit controls all, regardless of whether the cotton seller is loyal or rebel, or whether he is paid in corn-meal or gunpowder. The officers of the army, in numerous instances, are believed to connive and share the profits, and thus the army itself is diverted from fighting the rebels to speculating in cotton; and steam-boats and wagons in the pay of the government, are set to gathering and carrying cotton, and the soldiers to loading cotton-trains and guarding them.

—Letter to William P. Kellogg, former Congressman from Illinois,
June 29, 1863

My belief is that the permanent estimate of what a general does in the field is fixed by the "cloud of witnesses" who have been with him in the field; and that relying on these, he who has the right needs not to fear.

—*Letter to Major General John McClernand,*
August 12, 1863

There are those who are dissatisfied with me. To such I would say: You desire peace; and you blame me that we do not have it. But how can we attain it? There are but three conceivable ways. First, to suppress the rebellion by force of arms. This, I am trying to do. Are you for it? If you are, so far we are agreed. If you are not for it, a second way is, to give up the Union. I am against this. Are you for it? If you are, you should say so plainly. If you are not for force, nor yet for *dissolution*, there only remains some unimaginable *compromise*. I do not believe any compromise embracing the maintenance of the Union is now possible. All I learn leads to a directly opposite belief. The strength of the rebellion is its military—its army. That army dominates all the country and all the people within its range. Any offer of terms made by any man or men within that range, in opposition to that army, is simply nothing for the present; because such man or men have no power whatever to enforce their side of a compromise, if one were made with them.

—*Letter to James C. Conkling of Illinois, August 26, 1863*

Suppose refugees from the South, and peace men of the North, get together in convention, and frame and proclaim a compromise embracing a restoration of the Union; in what way can that compromise be used to keep Lee's army out of Pennsylvania? Meade's army can keep Lee's army out of Pennsylvania; and, I think, can ultimately drive it out of existence. But no paper compromise, to which the controllers of Lee's army are not agreed, can, at all, affect that army.

—*Letter to James C. Conkling of Illinois, August 26, 1863*

The signs look better. The Father of Waters again goes unvexed to the sea.

—Letter to James C. Conkling of Illinois on the Mississippi River being controlled now by the Union with Vicksburg having been taken, August 26, 1863

૭

Peace does not appear so distant as it did. I hope it will come soon, and come to stay; and so come as to be worth the keeping in all future time. It will then have been proved that, among free men, there can be no successful appeal from the ballot to the bullet; and that they who take such appeal are sure to lose their case, and pay the cost.

—Letter to James C. Conkling of Illinois, August 26, 1863

૭

You are a farmer, I believe; if not, you will understand me. Suppose you had a large cattle yard full of all sorts of cattle, cows, oxen, and bulls, and you kept selling and killing your cows and oxen, taking good care of your bulls. By and by you would find out you had nothing but a yard full of old bulls, good for nothing under heaven. Now it will be just so with my army if I don't stop making brigadier generals.

—Remark to a man soliciting another's promotion, September 14, 1863

૭

If the enemy's sixty thousand are sufficient to keep our ninety thousand away from Richmond, why, by the same rule, may not forty thousand of ours keep their sixty thousand away from Washington, leaving us fifty thousand to put to some other use? Having practically come to the mere defensive, it seems to be no economy at all to employ twice as many men for that object as are needed. With no object, certainly, to mislead myself, I can perceive no fault in this statement, unless we admit we are not the equal of the enemy man for man.

—Letter to Major General Henry W. Halleck, September 19, 1863

If our army can not fall upon the enemy and hurt him where he is, it is plain to me it can gain nothing by attempting to follow him over a succession of entrenched lines into a fortified city.
   —*Letter to Major General Henry W. Halleck, September 19, 1863*

❧

Were I to make a rule that in Missouri, disloyal men were outlawed and the rightful prey of good citizens, as soon as the rule should begin to be carried into effect, I would be overwhelmed with affidavits to prove that the first man killed under it was more loyal than the one who killed him. It is impossible to determine the question of the motives that govern men or to gain absolute knowledge of their sympathies.
   —*Remark to a delegation of "Radical Republicans" from Missouri and Kansas, September 29, 1863*

❧

The restoration of the Rebel States to the Union must rest upon the principle of civil and political equality of both races; and it must be sealed by general amnesty.
                   —*Letter to James Wadsworth, c. January 1864*

❧

When the war began three years ago, neither party, nor any man, expected it would last till now. Each looked for the end, in some way, long ere today. Neither did any anticipate that domestic slavery would be much affected by the war. But here we are; the war has not ended, and slavery has been much affected—how much needs not now to be recounted. So true it is that man proposes, and God disposes.
            —*Speech, Sanitary Fair, Baltimore, Maryland, April 18, 1864*

❧

Curtin, what do you think of those fellows in Wall Street who are gambling in gold at such a time as this? ... For my part, I wish every one of them had his devilish head shot off!
—*Remark to Pennsylvania Governor Andrew G. Curtin, April 25, 1864*

When my wife had her first baby, the doctor from time to time reported to me that everything was going on as well as could be expected under the circumstances. That satisfied me *he* was doing his best, but still I felt anxious to hear the first squall. It came at last, and I felt mightily relieved. I feel very much so about our army operations at this moment.

—Remark to a magazine writer, May 18, 1864

❧

War, at the best, is terrible, and this war of ours, in its magnitude and in its duration, is one of the most terrible. It has deranged business, totally in many localities, and partially in all localities. It has destroyed property and ruined homes; it has produced a national debt and taxation unprecedented, at least in this country. It has carried mourning to almost every home, until it can almost be said that the "heavens are hung in black."

—Speech, Great Central Sanitary Fair, Philadelphia,
June 16, 1864

❧

We accepted this war for an object, a worthy object, and the war will end when that object is attained. Under God, I hope it never will end until that time. Speaking of the present campaign, General Grant is reported to have said, "I am going through on this line if it takes all summer." This war has taken three years; it was begun or accepted upon the line of restoring the national authority over the whole national domain, and for the American people, as far as my knowledge enables me to speak, I say we are going through on this line if it takes three years more.

—Speech, Great Central Sanitary Fair, Philadelphia,
June 16, 1864

❧

I conceive that I may in an emergency do things on military grounds which cannot be done constitutionally by Congress.

—Remark to Senator Zachariah Chandler of Michigan,
July 4, 1864

I am sure you would not desire me to say, or to leave an inference, that I am ready, whenever convenient, to join in re-enslaving those who shall have served us in consideration of our promise. As matter of morals, could such treachery by any possibility escape the curses of Heaven, or of any good man? As matter of policy, to *announce* such a purpose would ruin the Union cause itself. All re-cruiting of colored men would instantly cease, and all colored men now in our service would instantly desert us. And rightfully too. Why should they give their lives for us with full notice of our purpose to betray them?

—*Letter to Charles D. Robinson, August 17, 1864*

Abandon all the posts now possessed by black men, surrender all these advantages to the enemy, and we would be compelled to abandon the war in three weeks.

—*Remark to Alexander Randall and Joseph Mills, August 19, 1864*

My enemies say I am now carrying on this war for the sole purpose of abolition. It is and will be carried on so long as I am President for the sole purpose of restoring the Union. But no human power can subdue this rebellion without using the Emancipation lever as I have done. Freedom has given us the control of 200,000 able-bodied men, born and raised on Southern soil. It will give us more yet. Just so much it has subtracted from the strength of our enemies, and instead of alienating the South from us, there evidences of a fraternal feeling growing up between our own and rebel soldiers. My enemies condemn my emancipation policy. Let them prove by the history of this war that we can restore the Union without it.

—*Remarks to Alexander Randall and Joseph Mills, August 19, 1864*

Much is being said about peace; and no man desires peace more ardently than I. Still, I am yet unprepared to give up the Union for a peace which, so achieved, could not be of much duration. The preservation of our Union was *not* the sole avowed object for which the war was commenced. It was commenced for precisely the reverse object—to destroy our Union. The insurgents commenced it by firing upon the Star of the West, and on Fort Sumter, and by other similar acts.

—Letter to Isaac Schermerhorn, September 12, 1864

❧

I wish all men to be free. I wish the material prosperity of the already free which I feel sure the extinction of slavery would bring. I wish to see, in process of disappearing, that only thing which ever could bring this nation to civil war.

—Letter to Henry Hoffman, October 10, 1864

❧

I can do nothing for you. ... I am under no obligation to provide for the wives of disloyal husbands.

—Remark to the wife of an imprisoned man,
November 2, 1864

❧

I feel how weak and fruitless must be any words of mine which should attempt to beguile you from the grief of a loss so overwhelming. But I cannot refrain from tendering to you the consolation that may be found in the thanks of the Republic they died to save.

—Letter to Mrs. Lydia Bixby, the mother of two sons killed in battle
(not five as Lincoln believed), November 21, 1864

❧

In stating a single condition of peace, I mean simply to say that the war will cease on the part of the government whenever it shall have ceased on the part of those who began it.

—Annual message to Congress, December 6, 1864

On careful consideration of all the evidence accessible it seems to me that no attempt at negotiation with the insurgent leader could result in any good. He would accept nothing short of severance of the Union—precisely what we will not and cannot give. His declarations to this effect are explicit and oft-repeated. He does not attempt to deceive us. He affords us no excuse to deceive ourselves. He cannot voluntarily reaccept the Union; we cannot voluntarily yield it. Between him and us the issue is distinct, simple, and inflexible. It is an issue which can only be tried by war, and decided by victory. If we yield, we are beaten; if the Southern people fail him, he is beaten.

—*Annual Message to Congress, December 6, 1864*

In presenting the abandonment of armed resistance to the national authority on the part of the insurgents, as the only indispensable condition to ending the war on the part of the government, I retract nothing heretofore said as to slavery. I repeat the declaration made a year ago, that "while I remain in my present position I shall not attempt to retract or modify the emancipation proclamation, nor shall I return to slavery any person who is free by the terms of that proclamation, or by any of the Acts of Congress." If the people should, by whatever mode or means, make it an Executive duty to re-enslave such persons, another, and not I, must be their instrument to perform it.

—*Annual Message to Congress, December 6, 1864*

Both parties deprecated war; but one of them would make war rather than let the nation survive; and the other would accept war rather than let it perish. And the war came.

—*Second Inaugural Address, March 4, 1865*

With malice toward none; with charity for all; with firmness in the right, as God gives us to see the right, let us strive on to finish the work we are in; to bind up the nation's wounds; to care for him who shall have borne the battle, and for his widow, and his orphan—to do all which may achieve and cherish a just and lasting peace, among ourselves, and with all nations.

—*Second Inaugural Address, March 4, 1865*

ॐ

I don't know why it is that I am troubled with these cases, but if I were, by interfering, to make a hole through which a kitten might pass, it would soon be large enough for the old cat to get through also.

—*Remark to a newspaper reporter after having been asked to waive conscription for a young man, March 21, 1865*

ॐ

My God, my God! Can't you spare more effusions of blood? We have had so much of it.

—*In conversation with Generals Grant and Sherman, on board the* River Queen, *when they told the President that Confederate General Robert E. Lee might have his Army of Northern Virginia fight one last battle, March 28, 1865*

ॐ

Thank God I have lived to see this. It seems to me that I have been dreaming a horrid dream for four years, and now the nightmare is gone.

—*Remark to Admiral David Porter, at the Union base on the James River, Virginia, April 3, 1865*

ॐ

They will never shoulder a musket again in anger, and if Grant is wise, he will leave them their guns to shoot crows with and their horses to plow with. It would do no harm.

—*Remark to Admiral David Porter, April 4, 1865*

ॐ

General Sheridan says, "If the thing is pressed I think that Lee will surrender." Let the *thing* be pressed.

—*Letter to Lt. General Ulysses S. Grant, April 7, 1865*

I have always thought "Dixie" one of the best tunes I have ever heard. Our adversaries over the way attempted to appropriate it, but I insisted yesterday that we fairly captured it. I presented the question to the Attorney General, and he gave it as his legal opinion that it is our lawful prize. I now request the band to favor me with its performance.

—Response to a serenade at the White House,
April 10, 1865

❧

The evacuation of Petersburg and Richmond, and the surrender of the principal insurgent army, give hope of a righteous and speedy peace whose joyous expression can not be restrained.

—Last speech, from a White House balcony, April 11, 1865

❧

I love the Southern people more than they love me. My desire is to restore the Union. I do not intend to hurt the hair of the head of a single man in the South if it can possibly be avoided.

—Remark to an Alabaman in Washington, D.C.,
on April 12, 1865

❧

His Generals

John C. Fremont

❧

I have great respect for General Fremont and his abilities, but the fact is that the pioneer in any movement is not generally the best man to carry that movement to a successful issue. It was so in old times, wasn't it? Moses began the emancipation of the Jews but didn't take Israel to the promised land after all. He had to make way for Joshua to complete the work. It looks as if the first reformer of a thing has to meet such a hard opposition and gets so battered and bespattered that afterward, when people find they have to accept his reform, they will accept it more easily from another man.

—Remark to an abolitionist delegation, January 25, 1863

ک

I thought well of Fremont. Even now I think well of his impulses. I only think he is the prey of wicked and designing men, and I think he has absolutely no military capacity.

—Remark to his assistant private secretary John Hay,
December 9, 1863

ک

He is like Jim Jett's brother. Jim used to say that his brother was the damndest scoundrel that ever lived, but in the infinite mercy of Providence he was also the damnedest fool.

—Remark to his assistant private secretary John Hay, on the rumor that Fremont would run against him for the Republican nomination for President, May 22, 1864

ک

Ulysses S. Grant

ک

I can't spare this man; he fights!

—Remark to Colonel Alexander McClure, who had urged the President to remove Grant from his command after the battle of Shiloh, April 1862

ک

What I want, and what the people want, is generals who will fight battles and win victories. Grant has done this, and I propose to stand by him.

—Remark to General John Thayer, in the midst of the outcry against Grant, c. April 1862

So Grant gets drunk, does he? ... Well, you needn't waste your
time getting proof; you just find out, to oblige me, what brand of
whiskey Grant drinks, because I want to send a barrel of it to each
one of my generals.
—*Remark to Grant's "particularly active detractors"; Grant, "at that pe-*
riod, was inflicting heavy damage upon the Confederates" (c. 1862)

ب

I have had stronger influence brought against Grant, praying for his
removal, since the battle of Pittsburg Landing, than for any other
object, coming too from good men; and now look at his campaign
since May 1. Where is anything in the Old World that equals it? It
stamps him as the greatest general of the age, if not of the world.
—*Remark to a newspaper reporter on Grant's Vicksburg campaign,*
May 29, 1863

ب

Grant here displayed about Vicksburg more generalship than ever
was shown by any general in America.
—*Remark to a Springfield acquaintance, Peter Van Bergen, 1863*

ب

If this Army of the Potomac was good for anything—if the officers
had anything in them—if the army had any legs, they could move
thirty thousand men down to Lynchburg and catch Longstreet. Can
anybody doubt if Grant were here in command that he would catch
him?
—*Remark to his secretary John Nicolay, December 7, 1863*

ب

Grant is the first general I've had. He's a general! ... You know
how it's been with all the rest. As soon as I put a man in command
of the army, he'd come to me with a plan of campaign and about
as much as say, "Now, I don't believe I can do it, but if you say so,
I'll try it on," and so put the responsibility of success or failure on
me. They all wanted me to be the general. Now, it isn't so with

Grant. … He doesn't ask me to do impossibilities for him, and he's the first general I've had that didn't!
　　　　　　　—Remark to the journalist William O. Stoddard (n.d.)

∾

General Grant is the most extraordinary man in command that I know of. I heard nothing direct from him and wrote to him to know why and whether I could do anything to promote his success, and Grant replied that he had tried to do the best he could with what he had; that he believed if he had more men and arms he could use them to good advantage and do more than he had done, but he supposed I had done and was doing all I could; that if I could do more he felt that I would do it.
　　　　　　　—Remark to Secretary of the Interior John P. Usher, 1864

∾

The nation's appreciation of what you have done, and its reliance upon you for what remains to do, in the existing great struggle, are now presented with this commission constituting you Lieutenant General in the Army of the United States. With this high honor devolves upon you also a corresponding responsibility. As the country herein trusts you, so, under God, it will sustain you.
　　　　　　　—Speech presenting Grant with his commission as Lieutenant-General,
　　　　　　　in the President's Cabinet chamber, March 9, 1864

∾

You and I, Mr. Stanton, have been trying to boss this job, and we have not succeeded very well with it. We have sent across the mountains for Mr. Grant, as Mrs. Grant calls him, to relieve us, and I think we had better leave him alone to do as he pleases.
　　　　　　　—Remark to Secretary of War Edwin Stanton (n.d.)

∾

Not expecting to see you again before the Spring campaign opens, I wish to express, in this way, my entire satisfaction with what you have done up to this time, so far as I understand it. The particulars of your plans I neither know nor seek to know. You are vigilant and self-reliant; and, pleased with this, I wish not to obtrude any restraints or constraints upon you. While I am very anxious that any great disaster, or capture of our men in great numbers, shall be avoided, I know that these points are less likely to escape your attention than they would mine.

—*Letter to Grant, at Army Headquarters, Culpeper Court House,*
Virginia, April 30, 1864

ە

Before Grant took command of the eastern forces we did not sleep at night here in Washington. We began to fear the rebels would take the capital, and once in possession of that, we feared that foreign countries might acknowledge the Confederacy. Nobody could foresee the evil that might come from the destruction of records and of property. But since Grant has assumed command on the Potomac, I have made up my mind that whatever it is possible to have done, Grant will do, and whatever he doesn't do, I don't believe is to be done. And now we sleep at night.

—*Remark to army chaplain John Eaton, 1864*

ە

I have seen your dispatch expressing your unwillingness to break your hold where you are. Neither am I willing. Hold on with a bulldog grip, and chew and choke as much as possible.

—*Telegram to Grant, August 17, 1864. (Reading this,*
Grant observed to staff members, "The President has
more nerve than any of his advisers.")

ە

If I had done as my Washington friends, who fight battles with their tongues instead of swords far from the enemy, demanded of me, Grant, who has proved himself so great a military captain, would never have been heard of again.

—*Remark to his friend from Illinois Ward Hill Lamon,*
early 1865

Joseph Hooker

❦

I think as much as you or any other man of Hooker, but I fear he gets excited.
  —*Remark to Secretary of the Navy Gideon Welles, late August 1862*

❦

I have placed you at the head of the Army of the Potomac. Of course I have done this upon what appear to me to be sufficient reasons. And yet I think it best for you to know that there are some things in regard to which, I am not quite satisfied with you. I believe you to be a brave and skilled soldier, which, of course, I like. I also believe you do not mix politics and your profession, in which you are right. You have confidence in yourself, which is a valuable, if not an indispensable quality. You are ambitious, which, within reasonable bounds, does good rather than harm. But I think that during General Burnside's command of the Army, you have taken counsel of your ambition, and thwarted him as much as you could, in which you did a great wrong to the country, and to a most meritorious and honorable brother officer. I have heard, in such way as to believe it, of your recently saying that both the Army and the Government needed a Dictator. Of course it was not for this, but in spite of it, that I have given you the command. ...
  And now, beware of rashness, but with energy and sleepless vigilance go forward and give us victories.
  —*Letter to Hooker, giving him command of the Army of the Potomac,*
January 26, 1863

❦

Have you already in your mind a plan wholly or partially formed? If you have, prosecute it without interference from me. If you have not, please inform me, so that I, incompetent as I may be, can try to assist in the formation of some plan for the Army.
  —*Letter to Hooker, May 7, 1863*

In one word, I would not take any risk of being entangled upon the river, like an ox jumped half over a fence, and liable to be torn by dogs, front and rear, without a fair chance to gore one way or kick the other. If Lee would come to my side of the river, I would keep on the same side and fight him, or act on the defense, according as might be my estimate of his strength relatively to my own.

—Letter to Hooker, June 5, 1863

I think Lee's Army, and not *Richmond*, is your true objective point. If he comes towards the Upper Peninsula, follow on his flank, and on the inside track, shortening your lines, whilst he lengthens his. Fight him when opportunity offers. If he stays where he is, fret him, and fret him.

—Telegram to Hooker, June 10, 1863. (Lee's Army of Northern Virginia had begun its invasion campaign, and Hooker, feeling helpless to stop the invasion, saw on the other hand an opportunity to take Richmond.)

If the head of Lee's army is at Martinsburg and the tail of it on the plank road between Fredericksburg and Chancellorsville, the animal must be very slim somewhere. Could you not break him?

—Telegram to Hooker, June 14, 1863

George B. McClellan

At the same time, General, you must not fight till you are ready. ... I have a notion to go out with you and stand or fall with the battle.

—Remark to George B. McClellan on the public's (and Lincoln's own) eagerness for military action, October 26, 1861

I will hold McClellan's horse if he will only bring us success.
—*Remark on McClellan's deliberate rudeness to him when Lincoln paid him a call, November 13, 1861*

∽

Why in tarnation ... couldn't the general have known whether a boat would go through that lock before he spent a million dollars getting them there? I am no engineer, but it seems to me that if I wished to know whether a boat would go through a ... lock, common sense would teach me to go and measure it. I am almost despairing at these results.
—*Remark to General Randolph Marcy, McClellan's father-in-law, on McClellan's plan to send boats up a Potomac River canal, February 27, 1862*

∽

One thing I can say, that the army will move, either under General McClellan or some other man, and that very soon.
—*Remark to Congressman James H. Campbell, March 3, 1862*

∽

We won't mention names, and I'll tell you how things are, state a proposition to you. Suppose a man whose profession it is to understand military matters is asked how long it will take him and what he requires to accomplish certain things, and when he has had all he asked and the time comes, he does nothing.
—*Remark to Virginia Woodbury Fox, wife of the assistant secretary to the Navy, on McClellan, March 7, 1862*

∽

... once more let me tell you, it is indispensable to *you* that you strike a blow. 1 am powerless to help this. You will do me the justice to remember I always insisted that going down the Bay in search of a field, instead of fighting at or near Manassas, was only shifting, and not surmounting, a difficulty—that we would find the same enemy and the same or equal intrenchments at either place. The country will not fail to note—is now noting—that the present hesitation to move upon an intrenched enemy is but the story of Manassas repeated.

I beg to assure you that I have never written you, or spoken to you, in greater kindness of feeling than now, nor with a fuller purpose to sustain you, so far as in my most anxious judgment I consistently can. *But you must act.*

—*Letter to McClellan, April 9, 1862*

૭

I think the time is near when you must either attack Richmond or give up the job and come to the defense of Washington.

—*Letter to McClellan, May 25, 1862*

૭

Save your army at all events. Will send reinforcements as fast as we can. Of course they can not reach you today, tomorrow, or next day. I have not said you were ungenerous for saying you needed reinforcement. I thought you were ungenerous in assuming that I did not send them as fast as I could. I feel any misfortune to you and your army quite as keenly as you feel it yourself. If you have had a drawn battle, or a repulse, it is the price we pay for the enemy not being in Washington, and the enemy concentrated on you; had we stripped Washington, he would have been upon us before the troops sent could have got to you.

—*Letter to McClellan, June 28, 1862*

૭

If, in your frequent mention of responsibility, you have the impression that I blame you for not doing more than you can, please be relieved of such impression. I only beg that in like manner you will not ask impossibilities of me. If you think you are not strong enough to take Richmond just now, I do not ask you to try just now. Save the Army, material and personnel; and I will strengthen it for the offensive again, as fast as I can.

—*Letter to McClellan, July 2, 1862*

McClellan knows this whole ground; his specialty is to defend; he is a good engineer, all admit; there is no better organizer; he can be trusted to act on the defensive; but having the slows, he is good for nothing for an onward movement.

—Remark to his cabinet on his having placed McClellan in command of Washington's defenses, September 2, 1862

ও

McClellan is working like a beaver. He seems to be aroused to doing something by the sort of snubbing he got last week. I am of the opinion that this public feeling against him will make it expedient to take important command from him. The cabinet yesterday were unanimous against him. They were all ready to denounce me for it, except Blair. He has acted badly in this matter, but we must use what tools we have. There is no man in the army who can man these fortifications and lick these troops of ours into shape half as well as he. … Unquestionably he has acted badly toward Pope. He wanted him to fail. That is unpardonable, but he is too useful just now to sacrifice.

—Remark to his assistant private secretary John Hay, September 5, 1862

ও

Well, gentlemen, for the organization of an army—to prepare it for the field—and for some other things, I will back General McClellan against any general of modern times—I don't know but of ancient times either—but I begin to believe that he will never get ready to fight.

—Remark to William O. Stoddard, a White House secretary (n.d.)

ও

Again, one of the standard maxims of war, as you know, is "to operate upon the enemy's communications as much as possible without exposing your own." You seem to act as if this applies *against* you, but can not apply in your *favor*. Change positions with the enemy, and think you not he would break your communication with Richmond within the next twenty-four hours?

You dread his going into Pennsylvania. But if he does so in full force, he gives up his communications to you absolutely, and you have nothing to do but to follow and ruin him; if he does so with less than full force, fall upon and beat what is left behind all the easier.

—*Letter to McClellan, October 13, 1862*

❦

Three times round and out is the rule in baseball. Stuart has been round twice around McClellan. The third time, by the rules of the game, he must surrender.

—*Remark to Adams S. Hill, of the* New York Tribune, *on Confederate General J. E. B. Stuart, who had twice led his cavalry around McClellan's Army of the Potomac, October 1862*

❦

You remember my speaking to you of what I called your overcautiousness. Are you not overcautious when you assume that you can not do what the enemy is constantly doing? Should you not claim to be at least his equal in prowess, and act upon the claim?

—*Letter to McClellan, October 13, 1862. (Lincoln urged McClellan to appreciate his army's advantages after the battle of Antietam and immediately attack.)*

❦

I have just read your dispatch about sore-tongued and fatigued horses. Will you pardon me for asking what the horses of your army have done since the battle of Antietam that fatigue anything?

—*Telegram to McClellan, October 25, 1862. (Two days later Lincoln apologized in a letter and explained his impatience with "five weeks of total inaction of the Army.")*

❦

I said I would remove him if he let Lee's army get away from him, and I must do so. He has got the "slows," Mr. Blair.

—*Remark to General Francis Blair, on McClellan, November 7, 1862*

By direction of the President of the United States, it is ordered that Major General McClellan be relieved from the command of the Army of the Potomac, and that Major General Burnside take the command of that army.

—*Orders to Major General Henry Halleck, which McClellan received November 7, 1862*

ം

This is the colonel who in the fall of 1861 tried to induce me to remove McClellan from the command of the army. At one time I thought I would have to arrest him for a traitorous conspiracy. ... Poor George, you knew him better than any of us. I did all I could for him but he could do nothing for himself.

—*Remark to Rush C. Hawkins, commander of the New York Volunteers, May 1864*

ം

Well, he doesn't know yet whether he will accept or decline. And he never will know. Somebody must do it for him. For, of all the men I have had to do with in my life, indecision is most strongly marked in General McClellan.

—*Remark to clergyman Joseph P. Thompson, on General George B. McClellan's consideration of taking the Democratic party's nomination for President, September 6, 1864*

ം

After the battle of Antietam, I went up to the field to try to get him to move and came back thinking he would move at once. But when I got home, he began to argue why he ought not to move. I peremptorily ordered him to advance. It was nineteen days before he put a man over the river. It was nine days longer before he got his army across, and then he stopped again, delaying on little pretexts of wanting this and that. I began to fear he was playing false— that he did not want to hurt the enemy. I saw how he could intercept the enemy on the way to Richmond. I determined to make that the test. If he let them get away I would remove him. He did so, and I relieved him.

—*Remark to his assistant private secretary John Hay, September 25, 1864*

George G. Meade

ও

"Drive the invaders from our soil"? My God! Is that all?
—*Remark on Meade's stated goal after the victory at Gettysburg, July 1863*

ও

We cannot blame him, Mr. Cameron; we cannot censure a man who has done so much because he did not do more.
—*Remark to Simon Cameron, Lincoln's former Secretary of War, shortly after Gettysburg, July 1863*

ও

We have certain information that Vicksburg surrendered to General Grant on the 4th of July. Now, if General Meade can complete his work, so gloriously prosecuted thus far, by the literal or substantial destruction of Lee's army, the rebellion will be over.
—*Letter to Major General Henry Halleck, on the battle of Gettysburg and its aftermath, July 7, 1863*

ও

They will be ready to fight a magnificent battle when there is no enemy there to fight.
—*Remark after reading Meade's telegraph message that the Army of the Potomac, having won at Gettysburg, would not be ready to attack Confederate General Robert E. Lee's fleeing army until the next day, July 12, 1863*

ও

Again, my dear general, I do not believe you appreciate the magnitude of the misfortune involved in Lee's escape. He was within your easy grasp, and to have closed upon him would, in connection with our other late successes, have ended the war. As it is, the war will be prolonged indefinitely. ... Your golden opportunity is gone, and I am distressed immeasurably because of it.
—*Letter, never sent, to Meade, July 14, 1863*

This is a dreadful reminiscence of McClellan. The same spirit that moved McClellan to claim a great victory because Pennsylvania and Maryland were safe. The hearts of ten million people sunk within them when McClellan raised that shout last fall. Will our generals never get that idea out of their heads? The whole country is our soil.

> —*Remark to his assistant private secretary John Hay on Meade's complacency with turning back and not defeating Lee's Army of Northern Virginia, July 14, 1863*

❧

Our army held the war in the hollow of their hand, and they would not close it. We had gone through all the labor of tilling and planting an enormous crop, and when it was ripe we did not harvest it. Still, I am very grateful to Meade for the great service he did at Gettysburg.

> —*In conversation with his assistant private secretary, John Hay, July 19, 1863*

❧

Well, to be candid, I have no faith that Meade will attack Lee; nothing looks like it to me. I believe he can never have another as good opportunity as that which he trifled away. Everything since has dragged with him. No, I don't believe he is going to fight.

> —*Remark to Secretary of the Navy Gideon Welles, July 26, 1863*

❧

Do you know, General, what your attitude toward Lee for a week after the battle reminded me of? … I'll be hanged if I could think of anything else than an old woman trying to shoo her geese across a creek.

> —*Remark to Meade on his lack of pursuit of Lee's Army of Northern Virginia, which, after Gettysburg, escaped across the Potomac, October 23, 1863*

William S. Rosecrans

୬

Truth to speak, I do not appreciate this matter of rank on paper, as you officers do. The world will not forget that you fought the battle of Stones River and it will never care a fig whether you rank General Grant on paper or he so ranks you.
—*Letter to Rosecrans, March 17, 1863*

୬

He is confused and stunned, like a duck hit on the head, ever since Chickamauga.
—*Remark to his assistant private secretary, John Hay, on Rosecrans, October 24, 1863. (Lincoln removed Rosecrans from his command of the Army of the Cumberland on October 19th.)*

୬

Philip H. Sheridan

୬

... how fortunate for the Secesh that Sheridan was a very little man. If he had been a large man, there is no knowing what he would have done with them.
—*Response to a serenade from a crowd celebrating Sheridan for his cavalry's series of victories in September and October, October 21, 1864*

୬

This Sheridan is a little Irishman, but he is a big fighter.
—*Remark to Annie Wittenmyer (n.d.)*

୬

General Sheridan, when this peculiar war began I thought a cavalryman should be at least six feet four inches high, but I have changed my mind. Five feet four will do in a pinch.
—*Remark to Sheridan, after his successful cavalry raid in northern Virginia, March 26, 1865*

William T. Sherman

❧

I know what hole he went in at, but I can't tell what hole he will come out of.

> —*Remark to General Sherman's brother, Senator John Sherman of Ohio, on the general's march through Georgia, early December 1864*

❧

Many, many thanks for your Christmas gift—the capture of Savannah.

> —*Letter to Sherman, December 26, 1864*

❧

A man once had taken the total abstinence pledge. When visiting a friend, he was invited to take a drink, but he declined, on the score of his pledge, when his friend suggested lemonade, which was accepted. In preparing the lemonade, the friend pointed to the brandy bottle, and said the lemonade would be more palatable if he were to pour in a little brandy; when his guest said, if he could do so "unbeknown" to him, he would "not object."

> —*Remark to Major Generals Ulysses S. Grant and William Tecumseh Sherman, answering Sherman's question of what was to be done with Confederate President Jefferson Davis when he was captured; "from which illustration," writes Sherman, "I inferred that Mr. Lincoln wanted Davis to escape, 'unbeknown' to him, and 'clear out' of the country, and the men composing the Confederate armies [to go] back to their homes, at work on their farms and shops," March 28, 1865*

❧

WOMEN AND MARRIAGE

I can never be reconciled to have the snow, rains, and storms to beat on her grave.

> —*Remark to a friend on Ann Rutledge, a woman he had loved who died in 1835*

Whatever woman may cast her lot with mine, should any ever do so, it is my intention to do all in my power to make her happy and contented; and there is nothing I can imagine that would make me more unhappy than to fail in the effort.
—*Letter to his fiancée Mary Owens, May 7, 1837*

൭

If you feel yourself in any degree bound to me, I am now willing to release you, provided you wish it; while, on the other hand, I am willing, and even anxious, to bind you faster, if I can be convinced that it will, in any considerable degree, add to your happiness. This, indeed, is the whole question with me. Nothing would make me more miserable than to believe you miserable—nothing more unhappy than to know you were so.
—*Letter to Mary Owens, August 16, 1837*

൭

Others have been made fools of by the girls; but this can never with truth be said of me. I most emphatically, in this instance, made a fool of myself. I have now come to the conclusion never again to think of marrying, and for this reason; I can never be satisfied with anyone who would be block-head enough to have me.
—*Letter to his friend Mrs. Eliza Browning, on his failed engagement to Mary Owens, April 1, 1838*

൭

I am now the most miserable man living. If what I feel were equally distributed to the whole human family, there would not be one cheerful face on the earth.
—*Letter to John T. Stuart, on Lincoln's broken engagement with Mary Todd, who later, in any case, became his wife, January 23, 1841*

൭

Nothing new here, except my marrying, which to me is a matter of profound wonder.
—*Letter to Samuel D. Marshall, November 11, 1842. (Lincoln married Mary Todd on November 4.)*

In this troublesome world, we are never quite satisfied. When you were here, I thought you hindered me some in attending to business; but now, having nothing but business—no variety—it has grown exceedingly tasteless to me. I hate to sit down and direct documents, and I hate to stay in this old room by myself.

—*Letter to his wife Mary, from Washington, D.C., where he was serving as a Congressman, April 16, 1848*

જી

Howdo! Howdo! I don't know how to talk to ladies.

—*Remark to a woman at an Illinois railroad station, c. mid-1850s*

જી

With pleasure I write my name in your album. Ere long some younger man will be more happy to confer *his* name upon *you*. Don't allow it, Mary, until fully assured that he is worthy of the happiness.

—*Note, autograph book of Mary Delahay, December 7, 1859*

જી

Your kind congratulatory letter, of August, was received in due course—and should have been answered sooner. The truth is I have never corresponded much with ladies; and hence I postpone writing letters to them, as a business which I do not understand. I can only say now I thank you for the good opinion you express of me, fearing, at the same time, I may not be able to maintain it through life.

—*Letter to Mrs. M. J. Green, September 22, 1860*

જી

So this is the little lady that all us folks in Washington like so much. Don't you ever come 'round here asking me to do some of those impossible things you women always ask for, for I would have to do it, and then I'd get into trouble.

—*Remark to the actress Rose Eytinge (n.d.)*

Little Sister, I hope you can come up and spend the summer with us at the Soldiers' Home. You and Mary love each other; it is good to have you with her. I feel worried about Mary; her nerves have gone to pieces; she cannot hide from me that the strain she has been under has been too much for her mental as well as her physical health.

　—*Remark to his wife's half-sister Emilie Todd Helm, December 1863*

Many a poor mother, Mary, has had to make this sacrifice and has given up every son she had—and lost them all.

　—*Remark to his wife on her anxiety about their son Robert going into the army, December 1863*

I am not accustomed to the use of language of eulogy; I have never studied the art of paying compliments to women; but I must say that if all that has been said by orators and poets since the creation of the world in praise of women were applied to the women of America, it would not do them justice for their conduct during this war. I will close by saying, God bless the women of America!

　—*Speech at the Sanitary Fair, Washington, D.C., March 18, 1864*

If you knew how little harm it does me and how much good it does her, you wouldn't wonder that I am meek.

　—*Remark to friends, on his wife Mary's having had her way in an argument, 1865*

APPENDIX

REMARKS ON ABRAHAM LINCOLN
BY HIS CONTEMPORARIES

Note: These are remarks made by people of Lincoln's time, most of whom knew well or at least had met Lincoln. Some are observations and criticisms spoken or written about Lincoln while he was alive, others in reflection after he was assassinated.

❧

... there entered, with a shambling, loose, irregular, almost unsteady gait, a tall, lank, lean man, considerably over six feet in height, with stooping shoulders, long pendulous arms, terminating in hands of extraordinary dimensions, which, however, were far exceeded in proportion by his feet. He was dressed in an ill-fitting, wrinkled suit of black, which put one in mind of an undertaker's uniform at a funeral; round his neck a rope of black silk was knotted in a large bulb, with flying ends projecting beyond the collar of his coat; his turned-down shirt-collar disclosed a sinewy muscular yellow neck, and above that, nestling in a great black mass of hair, bristling and compact like a ruff of mourning pins, rose the strange quaint face and head, covered with its thatch of wild, republican hair, of President Lincoln.

—William Howard Russell, British journalist, reporting for the
Times *of London, March 27, 1861*

❧

Mr. Lincoln does not have character enough for integrity and truth.
—Senator Stephen Douglas, debate at Ottawa, Illinois, August 21, 1858

I found the President better and younger-looking than his pictures. He is very dark and swarthy, and gives me the idea of a very honest, confiding, unsophisticated man, whose sincerity of purpose cannot be doubted.

—*John Lothrop Motley, American minister to the Austrian Empire,*
June 1861

❧

If he is 6 feet 4 inches high, he is only a dwarf in mind.

—*William Lloyd Garrison, editor of* The Liberator, *1861*

❧

The president is an idiot.

—*Letter by General George B. McClellan to his wife Ellen,*
August 19, 1861

❧

His intentions are excellent and he would have made an excellent President for quiet times. But this civil war imperatively demands a man of foresight, of prompt decision, of Jacksonian will and energy. These qualities may be latent in Lincoln, but do not yet come to daylight.

—*Count Adam Gurowski, diary, September 1861*

❧

I found "the original gorilla" about as intelligent as ever. What a specimen to be at the head of our affairs!

—*Letter by General George B. McClellan to his wife Ellen,*
November 17, 1861

❧

It is more and more evident that he is a man of very small caliber, and had better be at his old business of splitting rails than at the head of a government like ours, especially in such a crisis. He has evidently not a drop of anti-slavery blood in his veins; and he seems incapable of uttering a humane or generous sentiment respecting the enslaved millions in our land.

—William Lloyd Garrison, editor of The Liberator, *after Lincoln's first Annual Message, December 1861*

꙳

[Lincoln] does not act or talk or feel like the ruler of a great empire in a great crisis. ... He likes rather to talk and tell stories with all sorts of persons who come to him for all sorts of purposes than to give his mind to the noble and manly duties of his great post. It is not difficult to detect that this is the feeling of his cabinet.

—Richard Henry Dana, U.S. Attorney for Massachusetts (c. 1861–1862)

꙳

A frank, sincere, well-meaning man, with a lawyer's habit of mind, good clear statement of his fact, correct enough, not vulgar, as described; but with a sort of boyish cheerfulness, or that kind of sincerity and jolly good meaning that our class meetings on Commencement Days show, in telling our old stories over. When he has made his remark, he looks up at you with a great satisfaction, and shows all his white teeth, and laughs.

—Ralph Waldo Emerson, in his journal, on meeting the President, February 2, 1862

꙳

Lincoln belittles himself more and more. Whatever he does is under the pressure of events, under the pressure of public opinion. These agencies push Lincoln and slowly move him, notwithstanding his reluctant heaviness and his resistance.

—Count Adam Gurowski, diary, February 1862

꙳

How pitiable the attitude of President Lincoln, beseeching rebel States to do what God, justice, humanity, and our Constitution require *him* to do.

—George Cheever, letter, March 22, 1862

There are spots on the Sun. A blind man can see where the President's heart is. I read the spaces as well as the lines of that message. I see in them a brave man trying against great odds, to do right.

—*Frederick Douglass, speech, "The War and How to End It,"*
March 25, 1862

❧

I think Mr. Lincoln embodies singularly well the healthy American mind. He revolts at extreme measures, and moves in a steady way to the necessary end. He reads the signs of the times, and will never go faster than the people at his back. So his slowness seems like hesitation; but I have not a doubt, that when the people will it, he will declare that will, and with the disappearance of the only dissolvent [slavery], the dissolution of the union will be made impossible.

—*John Lothrop Motley, American minister to the Austrian Empire,*
June 22, 1862

❧

It is the strangest and yet the fittest thing in the jumble of human vicissitudes, that he, out of so many millions, unlooked for, unselected by any intelligible process that could be based upon his genuine qualities, unknown to those who chose him, and unsuspected of what endowments may adapt him for his tremendous responsibility, should have found the way open for him to fling his lank personality into the chair of state,—where, I presume, it was his first impulse to throw his legs on the council-table, and tell the Cabinet Ministers a story.

—*Nathaniel Hawthorne, novelist, "Chiefly about War Matters by a*
Peaceable Man," July 1862

❧

Will Lincoln be master of the opportunities, or will they escape him? Is he great enough for the time?

—*Charles Eliot Norton, July 1862*

He is not a genius; he is not a man like Fremont, to stamp the lava mass of the nation with an idea; he is not a man like Hunter, to coin his experience into ideas. I will tell you what he is. He is a first-rate *second-rate* man. He is one of the best specimens of a second-rate man, and he is honestly waiting, like any other servant, for the people to come and send him on any errand they wish.

—*Wendell Phillips, an abolitionist, "The Cabinet" speech,*
August 1, 1862

❦

We begin to lose faith in Uncle Abe.

—*George Templeton Strong, Treasurer of the United States Sanitary*
Commission, diary, August 4, 1862

❦

Abe Lincoln is not the style of goods we want just now ... it is impossible to resist the conviction that he is unequal to his place.

—*George Templeton Strong, diary, September 13, 1862*

❦

The most redoubtable decrees—which will always remain re-markable historical documents—flung by him at the enemy all look like, and are intended to look like, routine summonses sent by a lawyer to the lawyer of the opposing party. ... His latest proclama-tion, which is drafted in the same style, the manifesto abolishing slavery, is the most important document in American history since the establishment of the Union, tantamount to the tearing up of the old American Constitution.

—*Karl Marx, on the Preliminary Emancipation Proclamation, article in*
Die Presse, *a Viennese newspaper, October 12, 1862*

❦

It is a good thing he is fond of anecdotes and telling them for it relieves his spirits very much.

—*David Davis, judge from Illinois, November 1862*

... the President is not competent to write his own official papers.—It is evident that they are all from his pen; for they all bear the same marks of crudeness, incongruity, feebleness, and lack of method.

—*William Lloyd Garrison, editor of* The Liberator, *on the president's annual message, December 5, 1862*

❦

A man so manifestly without moral vision, so unsettled in his policy, so incompetent to lead, so destitute of hearty abhorrence of slavery, cannot be safely relied upon.

—*William Lloyd Garrison, editor of* The Liberator, *December 26, 1862*

❦

I think well of the President. He has a face like a hoosier Michael Angelo, so awful ugly it becomes beautiful, with its strange mouth, its deep cut, criss-cross lines, and its doughnut complexion. My notion is, too, that underneath his outside smutched mannerism, and stories from third-class county bar-rooms (it is his humor), Mr. Lincoln keeps a fountain of first-class practical telling wisdom.

—*Walt Whitman, letter, March 19–20, 1863*

❦

To say that he is ugly is nothing. To say that his figure is grotesque is to convey no adequate impression. Fancy a man six-foot, and thin out of proportion, with long bony arms and legs, which, somehow, seem to be always in the way, with large rugged hands, which grasp you like a vise when shaking yours, with a long scraggly neck, and a chest too narrow for the great arms hanging by its side; add to this figure a head, coconut-shaped and somewhat too small for such a stature, covered with a rough, uncombed and uncombable lank hair that stands out in every direction at once; a face furrowed, wrinkled and indented, as though it had been scarred by vitriol; a high narrow forehead; and, sunk deep beneath bushy eyebrows, two bright, somewhat dreamy eyes, that seemed to gaze through you without looking at you, a few irregular blotches of black bristly hair in the place where beard and whiskers ought to grow; a close-set, thin-lipped, stern mouth, with two rows of large white teeth; and a nose and ears, which have been taken by mistake from a head of twice the size.

—Edward Dicey, British journalist, 1863

❧

Unless you could give also the dry chuckle with which they are accompanied, and the gleam in the speaker's eye, as, with the action habitual to him, he rubs his hand down the side of his long leg, you must fail in conveying a true impression of their quaint humor.

—A "visitor" on Lincoln's anecdotes that had appeared in print (n.d.)

❧

Mr. Lincoln says he must laugh sometimes, or he would surely die.

—William O. Stoddard (n.d.)

❧

I can't trust your "Honest Old Abe." He is too smart for me.

—Horace Greeley, editor of the New York Tribune, *spring 1863*

❧

Who can see that man without losing all wish to be sharp upon him personally? Who can say he has not a good soul?

—Walt Whitman, letter, June 30, 1863

❧

... whatever may be said of his state-papers, as compared with the classic standards, it has been a fact that they have always been wonderfully well understood by the people, and that since the time of Washington, the state-papers of no President have more controlled the popular mind. And one reason for this is, that they have been informal and undiplomatic. They have more resembled a father's talks to his children than a state-paper. And they have had that relish and smack of the soil, that appeal to the simple human heart and head, which is a greater power in writing than the most artful devices of rhetoric. ... there are passages in his State papers that could not be better put—they are absolutely perfect. They are brief, condensed, intense, and with a power of insight and expression which make them worthy to be inscribed in letters of gold.

—Harriet Beecher Stowe, novelist, February 1864

❧

In times of our trouble Abraham Lincoln has had his turn of being the best abused man of our nation. Like Moses leading his Israel through the wilderness, he has seen the day when every man seemed ready to stone him, and yet, with simple, wiry, steady perseverance, he has held on, conscious of honest intentions, and looking to God for help.

—Harriet Beecher Stowe, novelist, February 1864

❧

He has not sought to control events, but he has known how to turn events, among the most important of which are to be reckoned the moods of a great people in time of trial, to the benefit of the nation and of mankind.

—Charles Eliot Norton, North American Review,
January 1865

❧

That rail-splitting lawyer is one of the wonders of the day. Once at Gettysburg and now again on a greater occasion he has shown a capacity for rising to the demands of the hour which we should not expect from orators or men of the schools. This inaugural strikes me in its grand simplicity and directness as being for all time the keynote of this war; in it, a people seemed to speak in the sublimely simple utterance of ruder times.

—Charles Francis Adams, Jr., letter to his father, the U.S. Minister to Great Britain, on the President's second inaugural speech, March 4, 1865

The President is dead. ... If he had been alive he would have been the first to call on me; but he has not been here, nor has he sent to know how I am, and there's the flag at half-mast.
—*Secretary of State William H. Seward, himself the victim of an assassination attempt, after reviving from his wounds, April 16, 1865*

ৎ

Certainly I have no special regard for Mr. Lincoln, but there are a great many men of whose end I would rather hear than his. I fear it will be disastrous to our people, and I regret it deeply.
—*Confederate President Jefferson Davis, April 19, 1865*

ৎ

Two dead men have killed slavery. What John Brown's death had initiated, Lincoln's death brought to completion.
—*Victor Hugo, French author, notebook, 1865*

ৎ

Abe was a good boy: he didn't like physical labor—was diligent for knowledge—wished to know and if pains and labor would get it he was sure to get it. He was the best boy I ever saw.
—*Sarah Bush Johnston Lincoln, his stepmother, September 1865*

ৎ

Abe, when old folks were at our house, was a silent and attentive observer—never speaking or asking questions till they were gone and then he must understand everything—even to the smallest thing—minutely and exactly. He would then repeat it over to himself again and again—sometimes in one form and then in another and when it was fixed in his mind to suit him he became easy and he never lost that fact or his understanding of it.
—*Sarah Bush Johnston Lincoln, his stepmother, September 1865*

ৎ

I did not want Abe to run for President—did not want him elected—was afraid somehow or other—felt it in my heart that something would happen to him and when he came down to see me after he was elected President I still felt that ... something would befall Abe and that I should see him no more. Abe and his father are in Heaven, I have no doubt, and I want to go there—go where they are.

—*Sarah Bush Johnston Lincoln, his stepmother, September 1865*

ॐ

Lincoln devoured all the books he could get or lay hands on: he was a constant and voracious reader.

—*John Hanks, his cousin, June 1865*

ॐ

I often said that God would not let any harm come of my husband. We had passed through five long, terrible, bloody years unscathed that I thought so—so did Mr. Lincoln: he was happy over that idea. He was cheerful—almost joyous as he got gradually to see the end of the war.

—*Mary Todd Lincoln, his wife, September 1866*

ॐ

Any man who took Lincoln for a simple-minded man would very soon wake up with his back in a ditch.

—*Leonard Swett, political ally, 1866*

ॐ

The force of his logic was in conveying to the minds of others the same clear and thorough analysis he had in his own, and if his own mind failed to be satisfied, he had no power to satisfy anybody else. His mode and force of argument was in stating how he had reasoned upon the subject and how he had come to his conclusion, rather than original reasoning to the hearer, and as the mind of the listener followed in the groove of his mind, his conclusions were adopted.

—*Leonard Swett, political ally, 1866*

From the commencement of his life to the close, I have sometimes doubted whether he ever asked anybody's advice about anything. He would listen to everybody; he would hear everybody, but he never asked for opinions. I never knew him in trying a lawsuit to ask the advice of any lawyer he was associated with. As a politician and as a President he arrived at all his conclusions from his own reflections, and when his opinion was once formed he never had any doubt but what it was right.

—*Leonard Swett, political ally, 1866*

ʕ

He did not seek company but when he was in it he was the most entertaining person I ever knew.

—*Joseph Gillespie, since 1832 a friend and colleague, 1866*

ʕ

He was the most indulgent parent I ever knew. His children literally ran over him and he was powerless to withstand their importunities.

—*Joseph Gillespie, since 1832 a friend and colleague, 1866*

ʕ

Mr. Lincoln had the appearance of being a slow thinker. My impression is that he was not so slow as he was careful. He never liked to put forth a proposition without revolving it over in his own mind, but when he was compelled to act promptly, as in debate, he was quick enough.

—*Joseph Gillespie, since 1832 a friend and colleague, 1866*

ʕ

There was a tinge of sadness in Mr. Lincoln's composition. He was not naturally disposed to look on the bright side of the picture. He felt very strongly that there was more of discomfort than real happiness in human existence under the most favorable circumstances, and the general current of his reflections was in that channel. He never obtruded these views upon others, but on the contrary strove as much as possible to be gay and lively.

—*Joseph Gillespie, since 1832 a friend and colleague, 1866*

෬

Men often called upon him for the pleasure of listening to him. I have heard the reply to an invitation to attend the theater, "No, I am going up to the White House. I would rather hear Lincoln talk for half an hour than attend the best theater in the world."

—*Isaac Arnold, his friend and political ally, 1869*

෬

The Union with him in sentiment rose to the sublimity of a religious mysticism.

—*Alexander H. Stephens, former vice president of the Confederacy, in his* A Constitutional View of the Late War between the States, *1870*

෬

As a lawyer, after his first year, he was acknowledged among the best in the state. His analytical powers were marvelous. He always resolved every question into its primary elements, and gave up every point on his own side that did not seem to be invulnerable. One would think, to hear him present his case in court, he was giving his case away. He would concede point after point to his adversary until it would seem his case was conceded entirely away. But he always reserved a point upon which he claimed a decision in his favor, and his concession magnified the strength of his claim. He rarely failed in gaining his cases in court.

—*Joshua Speed, one of his best friends, 1884*

෬

I never saw a more thoughtful face, I never saw a more dignified face, I never saw so sad a face. He had humor of which he was totally unconscious, but it was not frivolity. He said wonderfully witty things, but never from a desire to be witty. His wit was entirely illustrative. He used it because, and only because, at times he could say more in this way and better illustrate the idea with which he was pregnant. He never cared how he made a point so that he made it, and he never told a story for the mere sake of telling a story. When he did it, it was for the purpose of illustrating and making clear a point.

> —*David R. Locke ("Petroleum V. Nasby"), humorist, of his first meeting with Lincoln (in October 1858), 1886*

ॐ

… Lincoln, almost a giant in physical stature and strength, combined in his intellectual nature a masculine courage and power of logic with an ideal sensitiveness of conscience and a sentimental tenderness as delicate as a woman's.

> —*John Nicolay and John Hay, his private secretaries, 1886*

ॐ

In all my interviews with Mr. Lincoln I was impressed with his entire freedom from popular prejudice against the colored race. He was the first great man that I talked with in the United States, who in no single instance reminded me of the difference between himself and myself, or the difference of color, and I thought that all the more remarkable because he came from a State where there were black laws. I account partially for his kindness to me because of the similarity with which I had fought my way up, we both starting at the lowest round of the ladder. I must say this for Mr. Lincoln, that whenever I met him he was in a very serious mood. I heard of those stories he used to tell, but he never told me a story.

> —*Frederick Douglass, abolitionist, 1886*

ॐ

There was one thing concerning Lincoln that I was impressed with, and that was that a statement of his was an argument more convincing than any amount of logic. He had a happy faculty for stating a proposition, of stating it so that it needed no argument. It was a rough kind of reasoning, but it went right to the point. Then, too, there was another feeling that I had with reference to him, and that was that while I felt in his presence I was in the presence of a very great man, as great as the greatest, I felt as though I could go and put my hand on him if I wanted to, to put my hand on his shoulder. Of course I did not do it, but I felt that I could. I felt as though I was in the presence of a big brother, and that there was safety in his atmosphere.

—Frederick Douglass, abolitionist, 1886

୭

His great mission was to accomplish two things; first, to save his country from dismemberment and ruin; and second, to free his country from the great crime of slavery. To do one or the other, or both, he must have the earnest sympathy and the powerful co-operation of his loyal fellow-men. Without this primary and essential condition to success his efforts must have been vain and utterly fruitless. Had he put the abolition of slavery before the salvation of the Union, he would have inevitably driven from him a powerful class of the American people, and rendered resistance to rebellion impossible. Viewed from the genuine abolition ground, Mr. Lincoln seemed tardy, cold, dull, and indifferent; but, measuring him by the sentiment of his country, a sentiment he was bound as a statesman to consult, he was swift, zealous, radical, and determined.

—Frederick Douglass, abolitionist, 1888

୭

He was a profound believer in his own fixity of purpose, and took pride in saying that his long deliberations made it possible for him to stand by his own acts when they were once resolved upon.

—Noah Brooks, journalist, 1888

୭

He exercised no government of any kind over his household. His children did much as they pleased. Many of their antics he approved, and he restrained them in nothing. He never reproved them or gave them a fatherly frown. He was the most indulgent parent I have ever known. He was in the habit, when at home on Sunday, of bringing his two boys, Willie and Thomas—or "Tad"—

down to the office to remain while his wife attended church. He seldom accompanied her there. The boys were absolutely unrestrained in their amusement. If they pulled down all the books from the shelves, bent the points of all the pens, overturned inkstands, scattered law papers over the floor, or threw the pencils in the spittoon, it never disturbed the serenity of their father's good nature. ... Had they s—t in Lincoln's hat and rubbed it on his boots, he would have laughed and thought it smart.

—*William H. Herndon, his law partner, 1889*

ଔ

He probably had as little taste about dress and attire as anybody that ever was born: he simply wore clothes because it was needful and customary; whether they fitted or looked well was entirely above, or beneath, his comprehension.

—*Henry Clay Whitney, fellow Illinois lawyer, 1892*

ଔ

He *always* had a reply, and it was *always* pertinent, and frequently irresistibly funny, but the pity is that his funniest stories don't circulate in polite society or get embalmed in type.

—*Henry Clay Whitney, fellow Illinois lawyer, 1892*

ଔ

He had vast capacity for work, and also the exceedingly valuable faculty of putting work upon others. He could load, up to their limit or beyond it, his cabinet officers, generals, legislative supporters, and so forth. He could hold them responsible, sharply; but he never really interfered with them, "bothered them," at their work, or found undue fault with its execution.

—*William O. Stoddard, White House clerk, 1895*

ଔ

This unerring judgment, this patience which waited and which knew when the right time had arrived, is an intellectual quality that I do not find exercised upon any such scale and with such absolute precision by any other man in history. It proves Abraham Lincoln to have been intellectually one of the greatest of rulers. If we look through the record of great men, where is there one to be placed beside him?

—*Charles A. Dana, Assistant Secretary of War, 1898*

❧

When, in a tone of perfect ingenuousness, he asked me—a young beginner in politics—what I thought about this and that, I should have felt myself very much honored by his confidence, had he permitted me to regard him as a great man. But he talked in so simple and familiar a strain, and his manner and homely phrases were so absolutely free from any semblance of self-consciousness or pretension to superiority, that I soon felt as if I had known him all my life and we had long been close friends. He interspersed our conversation with all sorts of quaint stories, each of which had a witty point applicable to the subject in hand, and not seldom concluding an argument in such a manner that nothing more was to be said.

—*Carl Schurz, German-American general and politician, 1909*

❧

He was a very deliberate writer, anything but rapid. I cannot remember any peculiarity about his posture; he wrote sitting at a table and, as I remember, in an ordinary posture. As to dictation, I never saw him dictate to anyone, and it certainly was not his practice to do so. He seemed to think nothing of the labor of writing personally and was accustomed to make many scraps of notes and memoranda. In writing a careful letter, he first wrote it himself, then corrected it, and then rewrote the corrected version himself.

—*Robert Todd Lincoln, his oldest son, 1918*

❧

Among the many accusations which in hours of ill-luck have been thrown out upon Lincoln, it is remarkable that he has never been called self-seeking, or selfish. When we were troubled and sat in darkness, and looked doubtfully towards the presidential chair, it was never that we doubted the goodwill of our pilot—only the clearness of his eyesight. But Almighty God has granted to him that clearness of vision which he gives to the true-hearted, and enabled him to set his honest foot in that promised land of freedom which is to be the patrimony of all men, black and white—and from henceforth nations shall rise up to call him blessed.

—*Harriet Beecher Stowe, novelist, February 1864*

&

Now he belongs to the ages.

—*Edwin Stanton, Secretary of War, at Lincoln's bedside as the President died, April 15, 1865*

BIBLIOGRAPHY

Roy P. Basler, editor. *Abraham Lincoln: His Speeches and Writings*. Cleveland, Ohio: World Publishing Company, 1946.

Roy P. Basler, editor. *The Collected Works of Abraham Lincoln*. Volumes 1–8. The Abraham Lincoln Association. Springfield, Illinois, and New Brunswick, New Jersey: Rutgers University Press, 1953–1955.

Bob Blaisdell, editor. *The Civil War: A Book of Quotations*. Mineola, New York: Dover, 2004.

David Herbert Donald. *Lincoln*. Simon and Schuster, 1995.

Don E. Fehrenbacher, editor. *Abraham Lincoln: A Documentary Portrait Through His Speeches and Writings*. Stanford, California: Stanford University Press, 1964.

Don E. Fehrenbacher and Virginia Fehrenbacher, editors. *Recollected Words of Abraham Lincoln*. Stanford, California: Stanford University Press, 1996.

John Grafton, editor. *Great Speeches: Abraham Lincoln*. Mineola, New York: Dover, 1991.

Francis V. Greene. "Lincoln as Commander-in-Chief." *Scribner's Magazine*. Volume 46, 1909.

Harold Holzer. *Emancipating Lincoln*. Cambridge, Massachusetts: Harvard University Press, 2012.

Harold Holzer, editor. *Lincoln as I Knew Him: Gossip, Tributes and Revelations from His Best Friends and Worst Enemies*. Chapel Hill, North Carolina: Algonquin Books of Chapel Hill, 1999.

Harold Holzer, editor. *The Lincoln-Douglas Debates*. New York: Fordham University Press, 2004.

Louis P. Masur. *Lincoln's Hundred Days: The Emancipation Proclamation and the War for the Union*. Cambridge, MA: Belknap Press of Harvard University Press, 2012.

Alexander K. McClure, editor. *"Abe" Lincoln's Yarns and Stories: A Complete Collection of the Funny and Witty Anecdotes That Made Lincoln Famous as America's Greatest Story Teller.* Philadelphia: Henry Neil, 1901.

James M. McPherson. *The Struggle for Equality.* Princeton, New Jersey: Princeton University Press, 1995.

James M. McPherson. *Tried by War: Abraham Lincoln as Commander in Chief.* New York: The Penguin Press, 2008.

Wendell Phillips. *Speeches, Lectures, and Letters.* Boston: Lee and Shepard, 1884.

Allen Thorndike Rice, editor. *Reminiscences of Abraham Lincoln by Distinguished Men of His Time.* New York: North American Publishing Company, 1886.

Carl Schurz. *The Reminiscences of Carl Schurz, Volume 2: 1852–1863.* London: John Murray, 1909.

Walter Stahr. *Seward: Lincoln's Indispensable Man.* New York: Simon and Schuster, 2012.

Harriet Beecher Stowe. "Abraham Lincoln." *The Living Age.* Volume 80, February 1864.

Walt Whitman. *Selected Letters of Walt Whitman.* Edited by Edwin Haviland Miller. Iowa City: University of Iowa Press, 1990.

Douglas L. Wilson. *Lincoln's Sword: The Presidency and the Power of Words.* New York: Alfred A. Knopf, 2006.

Paul Zall, editor. *Abe Lincoln Laughing: Humorous Anecdotes from Original Sources by and about Abraham Lincoln.* Knoxville, Tennessee: University of Tennessee Press, 1995.